On Condition

Functional Training for Kung Fu

Bill Dowding

DEDICATION

To my Sifu,
The man who taught me the real kung fu:

Barry Lee
The Machine.

Contents

ACKNOWLEDGMENTS

First, to Barry Lee, my Sifu.
To my Sigung, the legendary Wong Shun Leung, who passed on the knowledge in the right way when so many wouldn't or couldn't.

Then to my Sihings; Fu Yang, Theo Pasialis, Gino Torreblanca and all those others I've trained with at the Barry Lee Ving Tsun Martial Arts Academy over the years and decades.

To my many students ever since I started teaching so long ago, especially those who learned more about exercise and fitness than I taught.

Thereafter, to the many, many people with whom I have trained, talked, shared and learned everything to do with not just this martial art, but martial arts in general as well all over the world, from Australia, to China, throughout Europe. Wisdom is everywhere. Go find it.

There are so many others, I can't list them all.

Thank you all.
Thank you very much.

Also, thanks to Scott Nightingale for his attention to graphics and help in fixing my photography.

And to my brother-out-law, Kevin Rees, for his black-belt level layout and his master level proofreading.

Any mistakes are mine.

"It is exercise alone that supports the spirit, and keeps the mind in vigour."

~ Marcus Tullius Cicero.

Part One

Introduction

"We are what we repeatedly do. Excellence then, is not an act, but a habit."

~ Aristotle, Ancient Greek Philospher.

Exercises are an important part of Ving Tsun Kuen (VTK), or indeed any martial art. Traditionally, Ving Tsun Kuen didn't have a warm-up as such, but nonetheless it had a program of exercises to strengthen and stretch the muscles, tendons, and joints in ways that would assist the student cope with progressively more arduous training, and strengthen the body in preparation for the stress of the maximal exertion in fighting. Much of it was directly descended from Shaolin, and much of that was based on the ancestral form that led to modern Yoga, combined with native Chinese exercises developed by Chinese doctors around the time of Christ. Exercises of this nature have a long and respectable tradition.

These exercises are often neglected, or worse, forgotten and labelled as unnecessary, but they are needed now more than ever with today's students. People are no longer fit and used to working hard all day, but spending much of their time behind a desk instead of behind a plough, in front of a computer rather than digging a ditch or harvesting rice.

Recent studies show that not only do we do insufficient exercise in our daily lives, but even those that do, don't do it in the right way or the right amounts anyway, so even those that we call fit, are not conditioned even like ordinary people 100 years ago, let alone fighters and warriors that many think we are trying to be. Modern Sports Science is undergoing a revolution in this area at the time of writing, with new discoveries in the way the body really works, which contradicts much of what is thought to be true. Our hunter instincts, which want us to be fit and work hard, are at variance with our stronger Primate instincts, which are to eat and sleep as much as possible. We need to strengthen our hunter instincts, and those of our students.

Once, the Sifu would look at a student and think, hmmm, this guy needs to be able to get his elbow in more, or maybe more stretch for the legs or more power for the punch. The Sifu would then assign the right exercise to that individual to remedy his lack of physical development in that specific area. Other aspects of his conditioning, through his daily life, were already adequate, or needed minimal work, which would be forthcoming during normal training. These days, though, everyone is unfit and weak compared to those of yesteryear.

In accordance with this, the traditional exercises are grouped into a warm-up designed for the beginning of class, instead of spread throughout training to be applied as needed, as they used to be originally.

The traditional VTK (Ving Tsun Kuen, also known as Wing Chun and many other spellings) exercises have also been augmented from other sources such as traditional Shaolin Kung Fu and other martial arts, and from modern exercise programs as well. Exercise is necessary for most people these days, and often required by governments or other bodies as part of licensing for exercise or sports programs, often needed for insurance, and exercise programs are even expected by students who join a school or class not only to learn to fight, but often also for fitness.

This series of exercises covers the full range of body movements in a short space of time with a minimum number of exercises. It is a simplified programmed entirely based on what we were taught by Sifu Barry Lee in the late eighties and early nineties as part of his much more comprehensive exercise program. Since we don't have an hour each day to do the whole program and most people don't have the time or energy to do both the fitness program and then train Ving Tsun Kuen for several hours, this has been shortened somewhat, while retaining the essence and the same kind of variety and broad range of movements, conditioning and fitness needed. I have included variations and more exercises than is needed in the warm up to give variety and more depth for those that are not sufficiently challenged by the shortened version. I have also dropped a couple of exercises we used to do regularly due to risk of injury, such as the plough, and some difficult and risky stretches like the bridge, although I include it here for those that want to go a bit further. I do plan on adding those exercises later in maybe a second book or a section in a later edition, simply for completeness, in a section I'll probably call "risky training" or some such.

One added benefit of this program is that the exercises are mindful. That is, you can't just do them, you must think about them. They are sufficiently different from other exercises in other programs that they must be learned and practiced. This means that you must focus on them, and this helps the student to focus on the training, and forget about what kind of a day he had. They are all open ended too, which means that no matter how good you are at them, you can do it better, harder, further or just simply more.

When I used to train with Sifu Barry Lee, we used to do a lot of exercises, about 40 minutes of blisteringly paced drills and exercises. This would follow a common format, but he would change specific exercises according to need, to avoid boredom, and simply to train things we hadn't done in a while. Typically, jumping on the spot would be 7 minutes and we would do three sets of each drill where here I use single sets for the most part. Floor exercises would involve at least a half dozen different kinds of crunches and sit ups of various kinds, and the Sun Asana section would involve 5 slow and 5 fast ones, and usually at least 5 or so more with variations.

It was gruelling.

However, it is not necessary to overdo it at the start. You can build up to it. Once you can do the given list at the back in about 10 minutes plus the time spent jumping on the spot, then you can start adding to the program. I will later release a video to follow along so the student can feel the pace. Even the video will be medium paced, and not as fast as it can be for those at more advanced level.

Modifying the exercise program accordingly can allow for all these situations.

All the exercises are open-ended and can also be modified upwards for those of increased fitness or flexibility (or decreased for that matter for injured, older, unfit or damaged people), so that it is a workout at all levels, once fully understood.

You can start easy, maybe taking half an hour to do the list at the end, and then over time make it very hard indeed simply by doing it in a shorter period until you get it down to about 10 or 15 minutes not stopping for a second. At that time, you can add more. Many of the exercises have variants and versions so the student or teacher can vary them according to need.

This book assumes a few things. It was written mostly so the teacher can see how to do it correctly, and illustrate some of these errors and risks and compensate for them, to reduce risk, or to modify the exercise for people at risk, or increase it for those with extra fitness or flexibility or strength, or to lead people with reduced strength, suppleness or flexibility to gain those facets to the point they can do the full exercise in its entirety as it is meant to be.

This book also assumes you know the basic Yee Chi Kim Yeung Ma or training stance. For details on this stance, and other basic techniques, see the appropriate documents or videos. Stance is a large topic on its own, and a very important issue in training. This book also assumes you already know things like the basic stances for moving and punches, and basic techniques of VTK, and focusses on the exercises themselves. While extremely important this is not the place to discuss these things. For the purposes of exercises, the precise stance is not vital anyway, just preferred.

Most of these exercises were done during 'warm up' and others were done at the end of training as part of a cool down. Others were spread throughout the training session.

There are many, many more exercises and drills as well used at various times, especially lots of stepping with and without partners, and also stepping fast, short explosive stepping, rapid closing the gap, moving through people and so on. However, this book has described the main exercise system we use at the beginning and end of class.

At the end of this book there is a suggested sequence, and there will soon be accompanying videos to show how it is done and the pace to follow along with the teacher.

Both the book and video are needed, but the book has WHY it is all done, and details that can't be seen in a video, and the video can show pace and what it looks like while in motion. The two completement each other and complete the exercise system, so both are needed. The biggest problem these days is that most will follow the video without the book and be led into error, with possible injury and incomplete training and understanding.

There are also many specific exercises at various levels for fixing problems or training certain techniques. These exercises are generally given by the sifu when appropriate, rather than to the class as a whole. These involve such elements as kicking (for example "Golden Rooster on One Leg" for strengthening the kick) or movement (Pivoting and Stepping drills) and preparation for various forms, such as drills for pole or knives. Other exercises exist such as to fix certain problems of students: such as rolling with both hands inside (to fix incorrect or badly completed Bong Sau) or outside (correcting Fook Sau) or the highly recommended Double Dan Chi Sau (also known as Cheung Sau) exercise, which fixes a very common problem of not enough of the correct forward force, especially for Tan Sau, elbow position for the punch and Fook Sau, Cheung Sau spearing force and really works on stance stability.

This book, being the first beginner's series of exercises, will not include this type of exercise.

This book is more for those people who do our particular system of VTK, through WSL and Barry Lee, but those others who wish to learn them or use them, they have great benefits for anyone wanting to do any version of Wing Chun, any other martial art, or simply to improve their own conditioning.

NOTE: As with any exercise program, if you have doubts about pre-existing injuries or conditions, you should consult both your Sifu and your doctor. Some exercises have some risk to newcomers, so the students must be watched carefully and taught properly so they don't injure themselves – particularly if they are middle aged or older, unfit and overweight, or if you are under 16 or so, or have any back, shoulder or knee problems.

Why Do Any Exercise?

"Our bodies are our gardens – our wills are our gardeners."

~ William Shakespeare, playwright.

I t is important for fighting that the student be able to endure maximum exertion for a short time, rather than long term endurance or indeed what normally passes for fitness such as jogging or running for several kilometres. These activities are good for general fitness, as is swimming, and are a valuable contribution towards a long and healthy life. Unfortunately, they have limited value to increase your ability to fight or train Ving Tsun Kuen. For this, something different is needed.

Fighting is very hard on the body, a great shock to the system physically as well as emotionally. The student needs to be strong enough to withstand this physical strain, especially the joints. Of more immediate importance, many of these exercises are critical and integral part of training, from the origins of Ving Tsun Kuen, and are not to be neglected if the student wants to learn the real Kung Fu. **Thinking of these exercises simply as 'warm up' is incorrect.** Not only does the student need to be fit and flexible enough to endure the training, they also need to strengthen and make flexible and supple the parts of the body needed for certain techniques, especially those involved with kicking. The training itself will eventually do that, but for a beginner, supplementary exercises are often needed, or at the very least, desirable. Also, it isn't a warm up if the next thing we do is hold a stationary stance for a long time immediately after the exercises. It would be counterproductive if that were the case. We would exercise AFTER the form. No reason not to, really, just I've found that in a class, people come late, and if the form was first, they would miss out on the most important part of training. So, virtually all schools do some manner of exercise first, then Siu Lim

Tao (SLT), our first form or first set. Siu Lim Tao also is an exercise system, for the mind and body, as well as many other things, but it is a static and slow one.

Fighting is not an activity that will need the same kind of fitness that you need in order to run a long way or lift weights in a gym. That is, unless you want to run away: Running away is not against the principles of Ving Tsun Kuen since only a fool will fight when there are other alternatives. You can get badly hurt even if you win, and you might lose even if you are better by happenstance, for example simply slipping on wet grass. However desirable for the rest of your life, this kind of fitness isn't absolutely necessary, but exercise is important both for warming up prior to training, getting a beginner moving, and developing the body ready for more advanced techniques, and strengthening weak areas of the student. It also begins the process of conditioning the mind to exertion. However, it is important to note that in a real fight there is no time for warm up, so a person should also condition their body to respond instantly from cold, rather than rely on when their body is best able to perform their Kung Fu.

Another point to note is that, as briefly mentioned earlier, although in many western countries warm-up is required by sporting regulations and/or insurance, these exercises are not really for warming up. Performing Siu Lim Tao after doing it would immediately negate any benefit, since SLT is slow and long, so you would cool down again. Doing something vigorous immediately after Siu Lim Tao, in fact, prepares your body for immediate response when cold, just like a real fight. Most of the exercises are more for increasing range of motion than muscle strength, for increasing joint strength, and more for training what is lacking in the day-to-day life of a student, rather than simply making muscles strong. They are also aimed at entire muscle complexes, rather than isolating muscles for strength such as gym exercises or weight training. This is especially true for the muscles that provide stability for joints, an area of strengthening vital in fighting and Kung Fu but often missed out in most normal fitness regimes, which operate on a basis of isolating muscles instead of muscle recruitment.

It has been noted that in recent times, many martial artists are suffering injuries from their training far worse than they would expect in a fight. BJJ guys are having back and neck and joint injuries, VTK guys knee, elbow and shoulder injuries, Aikido having wrist and knee injuries, TKD and Karate hip injuries, and so on. One important reason for this is that they are not physically conditioned to be able to take the strain of their techniques, of having them applied to themselves and of using their skills against each other, let alone in a fight. We are becoming soft. A comprehensive and focussed exercise program would help prevent a lot of these unnecessary injuries.

One question people ask is: If the old masters don't have exercises in Hong Kong or Foshan, why should we? One answer is, of course, you don't have to. However, if you want to improve your Ving Tsun Kuen to be the best you can be, then perhaps you should consider it. And of course, most do exercise, and did them when they were learning.

In the past, the students trained for at least four hours a day and often seven hours and worked hard at physical labour for a living the rest of the time. That is no longer the case. These days people typically train less than four hours a week, don't do any kind of heavy exertion otherwise, and work at a desk.

Something must make up the difference.

Also, contrary to popular belief, there are quite a few exercises that are traditionally part of Ving Tsun Kuen. The main ones for beginners are included in this book. They are not given in a particular order, except that they are grouped into categories. This is not the order that they are used in the exercises. They are divided into systems and groups for functionality.

After the exercises are presented, there is a list giving a suitable brief regime of the exercises, in an appropriate order, in the appendix. This of course can be varied at need and as desired.

Some of these exercises are from traditional Ving Tsun Kuen. Some are from Shaolin Kung Fu, some from other Martial Arts, including Karate and Boxing. Some are from traditional yoga used by Hindu wrestlers and Kalari Payat exponents. Others are from various sources, including African Masai warriors (This is the origin of the exercise "Jumping on the Spot" which essentially was to replace skipping or other similar exercises, but takes up less room).

Leading the Exercises

"The greatest leader is not necessarily the one who does the greatest things. He is the one that gets the people to do the greatest things."

~ Ronald Reagan, President of the United States of America.

First and foremost, the teacher should place emphasis that this is not really a warm-up, or rather not solely a warm-up, but also a series of strengthening exercises. Many countries require warm-ups for exercise programs, and Ving Tsun Kuen in many cases must comply. So, we call this a warm-up to satisfy legalities and other issues, but we must keep in mind that it is really an exercise program, somewhat separate from the Kung Fu style itself, but still necessary.

How you approach the exercises will be how you approach your Ving Tsun Kuen, which is how you will fight. **Therefore, they should not be done casually and superficially, but with full heart and intention**. Naturally, beginners should approach it carefully, and slowly, and take their time. They should learn each one, and discover how far you can push themselves in each one without injury. Once you get the shapes and structures right, they can then push it a little more as they learn how their body responds to each one, going as far as they can, safely. Then a little further as they progress. As strength and flexibility increases, the students should give more effort, doing it harder and faster step by step, until they are doing it as fast as they can. Some exercises will be easy for some people while others find them hard, and vice versa. Everyone is different. The natural thing to do is focus on the ones that are easy, but instead **the smart thing is to focus on the ones the student has trouble with**.

Junior students need help, first by teaching them the exercises correctly, and giving advice individually with each of these exercises, in order to learn them safely and well. The priority should be for them to learn the basic, easier versions as soon as possible so they can do their own exercises if they are late to class sometime in the future, or if the school has sessions where the students mind their own training, or they do some at home. The ones they have trouble with, modify them or teach them ways to accomplish them, but **always with the goal that they will eventually do them correctly and completely.** This is especially important for younger students, still growing. It is also important for those that have injuries, temporary or permanent, certain medical conditions, or are overweight or older students, or those whose builds are particularly weak or inflexible.

Safety is key. Beginners, older people, younger people, overweight people or those with other problems such as people with injuries or medical conditions have special needs and they should be encouraged, and challenged by the exercises, but not humiliated or injured by the difficulty. Some exercises are generally harder for men some generally harder for women. Although I certainly have had women instructors push fit men to their limits – and one of them was a sixteen-year-old girl. Likewise, some are easier. Be aware of which is which and watch for safety. If people injure themselves, then they are likely to resist doing the exercises later and make it harder for themselves to accomplish their goals. And these people are usually the ones who need it most.

Leading the exercises should be done with these points in mind. The pace should suit the students, with the most inexperienced ones being given the right pace, the right number of repetitions, and the right degree of difficulty. This takes experience and observation. The more experienced students can put more into the exercises on their own without being led – repetitions, range, variations etc. – while the beginners learn how to do them, as the experienced students should already know how. Caveat - the more experienced students should not do dangerous variations or exercises not on the beginners list or exercises outside the program where the new students can see them, so the new students aren't encouraged to take risks they should avoid.

If there are a few inexperienced students in the room with a large number of students, I usually have one or two people involved with leading the exercises, cooperating. This makes a team of three in a larger class. One is obviously the Sifu or head instructor or something like that. In medium classes, he can be the 'observer' as well, if it only needs two people. In very small classes the Sifu is leader, observer and teacher all in one. For the rest of the team, as follows: One I will call the leader. He is the one who performs the exercises and yells out the commands. The other is an observer. He walks around, watching and he is the one who should advise the beginner how to do the exercises individually, if they get stuck or get confused. I usually call this person "the coach" or "the observer" as appropriate. If they need to, the observer should let the rest of the exercises continue under the leader, while teaching the newcomer a limited number of the exercises, just one or two, or spend a bit of time with the student just correcting the part of one exercise he is having trouble with. This continues progressively – in each lesson, increase their knowledge until they can safely join the class in the exercises with the other students. Another senior can be designated to help one student with problems or take them out of the exercises and teach them individually, if there are multiple beginners.

No-one but the leader should talk during the exercises, unless the observer/instructor is needed, nor should anyone else give instruction except for those designated, in order to reduce confusion. The coaching guy should keep his voice low so as not to disturb the flow of the students. Management of this is crucial especially as beginners are easily confused. Best to let the leader lead, and allow the coach to coach, and the rest mind their own training, even if they want to help – don't let students help each other in this. People will try to help their friends who just started, and this is commendable, but it gets in the way. Tell them to mind their own training. They are both disturbing their own training and disturbing the class, and confuse the beginner, and may not be able to show the right thing anyway. They should mind their own training, and refrain from commenting on other's training. Even the observer should talk quietly, with only the person needing help being able to hear him.

The leader should use a clear, imperative voice, like a sergeant major in the military. "Do this, then do that!". Commands should be short, clear and repetitious, consistent from class to class and leader to leader, with every person who leads using the same words, the same labels and short descriptions, the same names for drills, and the same order as each other, to avoid confusion. Give the name of the drill before starting it, to teach the students the names. It doesn't matter if the names are not standard or the same from school to school, although it would be best to do so, if the schools are branches of the main school, so leaders from one school can help in another branch. The names just need to be something for the students to focus on. Don't let the leader say too much, usually, unless in a small class where he can talk more quietly to give some help or advice to a beginner. The leader should not break exercise to do this, should simply pause, give advice, continue without moving from where he is. Allow the coach to do his job.

Let the person coaching give more information for the beginners, and he should follow the leader, and cooperate with him. For example, if necessary, he can ask the leader to hold a position or exercise for a short time to allow the coach time to explain some steps, especially if there is risk of injury. This pausing should be short, and not too often. If it is too often, it is better to take the people having difficulty out of the group, and take them aside for closer work.

The observer/coach should speak only to the person needing help,.quietly if possible, to avoid confusing the other students. Use the leader as a demonstration model and point out the parts the student needs to take note of. It doesn't hurt to go over it a few times. Don't worry about the time, if the student needs to learn it, but do make sure that the other students don't suffer from holding one exercise too long etc. The Sifu can hurry people up if need be.

The leader needs to be able to do the exercises well enough to demonstrate, and the observer familiar with exercise safety and what to avoid etc. Often, I get the fitter guy to lead, and someone who is injured or not so physically capable, etc., but knowledgeable in the system to be the coach. It helps everyone then.

In classes where the students all know the basic versions at least, and no assistant/observer/instruction is needed, then the leader can run the class alone, and start to add variations as appropriate, increasing repetitions or increasing the pace, pushing the students to just a little better performance each time.

In other classes, I have regularly had one small group of beginners learning the exercises separately, letting the more advanced students do it themselves, or sometimes really being pushed hard by some very enthusiastic leader, and medium level guys being pushed along a little. It all depends on class size and the current needs of the students.

A note on naming the exercises: I have no idea what the Chinese names for many of these things are, and we just made up names so we could talk about them and give instructions. You can call them what you like, and if someone knows the real names, I'd be happy to learn them, but that isn't important. **Doing them right is important. Doing them at all is.** The exercises are not as important at the rest of the system, but these give students a leg up in the difficult climb to getting the actual Ving Tsun Kuen right by preparing them mentally and physically for it.

Part Two

Traditional Ving Tsun Kuen Exercises

This group of exercises are traditional in Ving Tsun Kuen and used to be taught in classes in HK in the old days. They were given to those students with certain problems, mostly to do with inability to put the elbow in the centre and hold it there.

In our school, we spread the traditional group throughout the training session from the beginning of the exercises, to the end of the warm up to maximize flexibility to the student in order to get closer to the ideal, and to allow them to catch their breath a bit from the hard exercises previously done. Others are spread throughout training, sometimes regularly, sometimes one-off type ones for interest or to emphasize a point or focus on an aspect of training for the day. Others are at the end in cool-down, for making the end of the class definite as well as expending the last bits of energy a person has in one exhausting finish to cap the lesson off.

I put these exercises first in this document not because they are the best or should be done first, but in order to showcase them and because they are important specifically for Ving Tsun Kuen and are not really found anywhere outside of Ving Tsun Kuen that I can determine.

The exercises will be described in detail, then followed by pictures going through each major point. Pictures and students nearly always have errors, so it is important to follow the descriptions if the student is slightly different.

Elbow Squeeze

This exercise is designed to strengthen the small muscle groups that hold the elbow in, and to get students to not use their hand and forearm for the appropriate techniques, but their elbow. This is to help with blocking, for example Jum and Fook Sau, and to increase the stability of the punch at impact.

For many, mostly adult men, this is extremely difficult exercise, and takes a lot of stretching and time to satisfactorily complete this exercise. There are many remedial stretches to help it along. This is due to the male shoulder and chest muscular development. Relaxing will help a lot here, but it is hard to relax and use the muscles at the same time.

1. First stand in a training stance. (Figure 1). Ensure that you remain upright and do not hunch your back or curve your chest. Keep the waist forwards the whole time and keep the stance strong and correct, with good upright posture.
2. Next, put your palms together with the fingers and forearms parallel to the ground and pointing forwards at the height of your solar plexus. (Figure 2). In the photo it looks like he is pointing slightly up, but this is due to the camera angle. The line of the fingers should be parallel to the ground. The elbows should be close in, as close to the ribs as possible. For thin people at this point it is not practical to have the elbows right against the body, but the force should be like you are trying to do that.
3. Keeping the hands together and horizontal, slowly push them forwards. The elbows should scrape along the sides of your body, staying firmly in contact with the body until they meet at your solar plexus. At that point, the whole forearm should be touching each other from fingertip to elbow, meeting in the centre of your body and parallel to the floor. (Figure 3).
   Now, continue to push forwards until your elbows are a fist and a thumb from your body, the forearms still parallel to the ground and elbows and hands squeezed together. The pressure should be on your elbows more than the hands. (Figure 4). Don't hunch or round the shoulders. They should remain square.
4. Once extended out to a fist and a thumb away from the centre of your body, still squeezing the elbows together, hold for ten seconds or longer.
5. Relax. Shake it out.
6. Repeat 2 more times.

7. Each time the movement going out should take at least a count of ten, and then hold for a count of ten.

This strengthens the muscles for techniques such as Jum Sau or Fook Sau and makes the punch more efficient.

Errors

1. Pushing the hands and not the elbows.
2. Rounding the shoulders. This should not happen. It is largely inevitable with bigger guys, but once the stretch is there, square the shoulders back again.
3. Hunching the back. Same as error 2 above.
4. Losing the waist. Keep it forward and pelvis tilted up.
5. Bending the back. Keep upright.
6. Not pushing the elbows out from the body or keeping them too close. They are supposed to go out a **fist-and-a-thumb** (not just a fist) distance from the centre, still squeezing.
7. Keeping the hands too high. This isn't that bad at the start as people learn the stretch, as it enables people to put the elbows together, especially in the early days of practicing the stretch. But then, you must lower the hands until they are level with the elbows, almost horizontal, in at least the 'Jum Sau' position. Having the hands start high is sometimes a suitable intermediate step for people who have difficulty with this exercise. They just have to start bringing the forearms parallel to the ground over time.

Intermediate Exercises

1. Try holding the elbow into the centre with the other hand and stretching it into place, then slowly taking the pressure off and holding the elbow into the centre with muscles alone.
2. Stretch the shoulder as a normal shoulder stretch, then while holding the elbow in place with the other arm or hand, turn the forearm in to Tan Sau. This helps stretch the muscles, limiting movement.
3. See the last point in "Errors" above for another intermediate exercise.

FIGURE 1

FIGURE 2

FIGURE 3

FIGURE 4

Arm Wrap

This is also for those people who have difficulty maintaining the Jum and Fook Sau position, which is most beginners. People usually either need the "Elbow Squeeze" exercise or this one for stretching it into place, and often both.

The intermediate stretches are the same as in the previous exercise, and all the postural errors and advice is identical. The main difference here is trying to sort out the hands and the direction of the grab. There is one more intermediate exercise for this, and that will be covered at the end.

1. Get into a training stance. (Figure 5). Ensure that you remain upright and do not hunch your back or curve your chest. Keep the waist forwards the whole time and keep the stance strong and correct. Maintain this posture throughout. This is the same as in the previous exercise.

2. Put your left arm out, elbow bent and close to the centre of your body, about a fist and a thumb from your solar plexus to your elbow. (Figure 6). It is pretty much a Fook or Jum Sau shape, although the hand should be level with the elbow, and not higher as in the technique. It is a good place to start, however, for those that already know the technique.

   Note: We start with the left arm first for the same reason that we do in Siu Lim Tao, in that we block mirror image and most people will be attacking with the right hand first. In this case, it doesn't really matter, but we try to be consistent through the entire of our training. This book is not the place for a complete explanation of these topics.

3. Place your right elbow behind your left elbow so that your arms are on the opposite sides of each other than they normally are. (Figure 7).

4. Turn your hand so that the outwards edge is downwards and flatten your hand so the fingers point forwards. Grab your wrist. (Figure 8).

5. Now push your arms forwards until your elbows are a fist-and-a-thumb from your solar plexus, and forearms are parallel to the ground. (Figure 9).

6. Hold for ten seconds.

7. Repeat on the right side.

8. Slowly shake out your arms.

Errors.

The most common errors for this one are the same as for the "Elbow Squeeze" above, plus where students don't get behind the elbow. There is often trouble for the student to sort their hands out, trying to grab backwards with their hand. The teacher may have to help a little, carefully so as not to injure the student, in sorting it out.

Intermediate Exercises.

The stretches for this are the same as well. There are a few intermediate exercises to help along.

First, don't grab the wrist if you can't reach it, grab the base of the thumb instead, even if you must bend the wrist to do it. Once you can grab it, straighten the wrist and pull the arms down to horizontal and force the rest into line. Over time, you will slowly be able to do it properly.

Second, don't grab the wrist at all, just push your hands in the direction of the thumbs, and hold. This will eventually stretch until you can go to the next phase, above.

Third, if you can't even do that, place your hand in the Tan Sau position, and pull your elbow towards centre with the other hand. Hold for 30 seconds, then change sides. Do this regularly, like 3 times a day, until you can do the above intermediate stretch, until you can do the exercise.

FIGURE 5

FIGURE 6

FIGURE 7

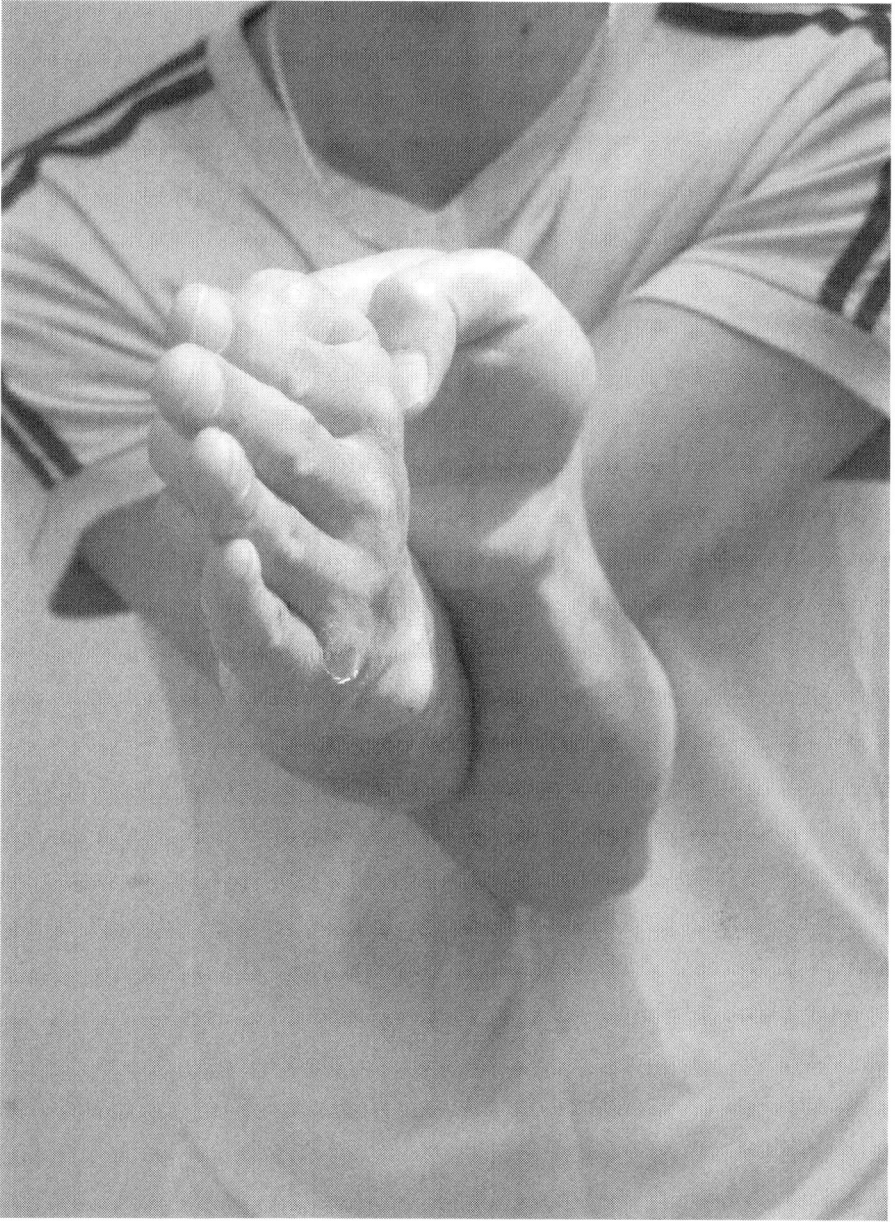

FIGURE 8

FIGURE 9

Arm Rotations

This is another traditional exercise, but it is also found in Shaolin and many other Kung Fu styles, including some Karate and Jiu Jitsu and so on.

Normally, for a basic class, we do ten forward rotations with both hands simultaneously, then ten backwards, also with both hands. This increases the strength and suppleness of the shoulders, and a powerful 'looseness' of the shoulders for punching, and the range of motion for Chi Sau and so on. It will strengthen muscle and bone attachments very well. It is also invaluable for getting the blood flowing through the shoulders when tired from punching or Chi Sau, reviving them, and thus enabling the student to continue training after they are tired from the first round of training.

This exercise can also be done one hand at a time and can be done heavily ballistic for the advanced students who want to increase this strength. For that, you need to get into a fighting stance (or even deeper for stability) rather than a training stance and use the hand on the same side the leg is back and do it with whirlwind force, ten or more times in each direction, then change hands and do it on the other side.

The hands should feel very heavy while you are doing it, and blood should rush to the hands and make the palms very red.

For those with shoulder issues, the basic two-handed exercise (or even one-handed) can be used slowly and loosely to increase mobility, but in this case it should be done carefully so as to cause no further aggravation of the student's condition.

Here I will cover the basic two-handed one. The other methods can be extrapolated, I am sure, from the given descriptions.

1. Get into a Yee Chi Kim Yeung Ma Training Stance. Please refer to Figure 1.
2. Keeping your elbows straight, take your elbows backwards and upwards past your ears and down, crossing left over right at the elbows.
3. Make sure you are going through a full range of motion and really open up your chest, breathing in. Follow the figures given below as you go through from figure 10 all the way through each figure up to figure 23.
4. Alternate each time around, crossing left over right, then right over left.
5. The arms should swing freely, and move quite quickly, so there is a slight tingling and pinkness in the hands.

6. After doing ten forwards, the cycle is reversed, repeating the motion, doing ten backwards like backstroke. Move the arms past the ears, behind the back, past the waist, back up crossing elbows, and so forth. When going backwards, turn the hands like a back-stroke swimmer, and keep the full range of motion going.

FIGURE 10

FIGURE 11

FIGURE 12

FIGURE 13

FIGURE 14

FIGURE 15

FIGURE 16

FIGURE 17

FIGURE 18

FIGURE 19

FIGURE 20

FIGURE 21

FIGURE 22

FIGURE 23

Knee Raises and Hindu Squats

These exercises increase the height of the kick, and teaches the student to be light of foot.

Normally, the student would do 50 knee raises followed immediately without pause with 20 squats. This would be called one set. For beginners, we usually do one set, but increase it to 3 sets as the student advances, once the student can do the whole basic sequence of the warm up with enough speed, power and skill.

With the Knee Raises, you need to at least bring the knees higher than the waist at minimum, preferably hitting yourself in the chest. And when you bring them down, you need to control the feet so you put the foot down as quietly as possible. This teaches control of the feet, something difficult to do, especially at speed. **This translates directly into fighting by being sure-footed and knowing where your feet are without looking. It is also important for kicking.**

Usually, you start the sequence of squats fairly slowly, kind of using it as a stretch and range of motion drill, especially if it is early in the day, to loosen the joints and muscles. Make sure you are doing the complete motion. After the first one or two, you start to increase the speed and power until you are going as fast as you can at about 10 or 20 knee raises, or about 5 or 10 squats, or about half way through. This is especially important with the squats as the synovial fluid in the knee needs time to warm up and become more plastic and lubricate the joint, especially in older people, people with injuries, or anyone sitting around all day instead of walking. After hitting maximum speed, keep that rate for the rest of the exercise, including the knee raises, and any further repetitions.

With the squats it is important to come down under control, so you don't impact your whole weight on the knee joint, again especially for injured people, or older or overweight. It is considered a high-risk exercise by sports science due to this, but since we need to make a whole range of motion, the suggested method of only going part way, which is safer, only builds muscle. This is not what we are trying to do here. On the way up, you need to fully straighten the legs. Full range of motion.

The back also needs to be as vertical as possible. Leaning forwards, which is instinctive, uses entirely different muscles and doesn't work on the ones needed for training. Ving Tsun Kuen has a vertical posture, so the exercises need to reflect this. By doing other ways, they do not directly translate to training, and so some of the benefit is lost. More on this when we talk about floor exercises.

These Hindu Squats are a variation used in Ving Tsun Kuen traditionally, and very similar to the ones used by Kalari practitioners among other types. There are several types of this around the world, and many are teaching it somewhat differently. Ours is a variant where we are flat footed and not swinging our arms, but keeping them in the Jum Sau position, due to our own needs in training.

At the end of these two exercises, especially if you do the full 3 reps, the loosening exercise "Ten Second Walk" can and perhaps should be done to shake out the legs and help them recover.

Knee Raises

First, we consider Knee Raises:

They are performed by raising the knee into the chest, then putting your foot down quietly, then quickly raising your other leg, and doing the same again. It should be done as fast as possible.

1. Hunch slightly forward with your feet a shoulder width apart, your hands slightly extended to the front, and elbows pushed forward.in the Jum Sau position (Figure 24).
2. Raise your knee so that it hits you in the chest firmly, making a noise. (Figure 25).
3. Bring your foot back to the ground lightly. (Figure 26). Don't slam it down, but under control even though you are going fast.
4. Now bring the other knee up and hit the centre of your chest (Figure 27).
5. Bring your foot down again lightly.
6. This brings the cycle back to the beginning. Do 50 knee raises, or 25 cycles of one leg each.

Putting your foot down lightly teaches you to control your feet so you can put them where you want to and to increase the efficiency in which you move your feet. By moving quietly, you decrease friction with the floor, thus move faster, and controlling how your feet hit the floor will prevent you from committing too much weight when you transfer from foot to foot, and will enable you to move more smoothly. Being quiet also helps confuse your enemy, because they don't know where you are, or even if you are moving.

Common errors involve not lifting both legs to the same height, not lifting the knees at least above the waist at a minimum, and slamming down the feet. Also "jogging" or running or bouncing type motions are to be avoided. It's not some weird running motion. The body should be held as still as possible, without bobbing or moving around. This teaches body control.

FIGURE 24

FIGURE 25

FIGURE 26

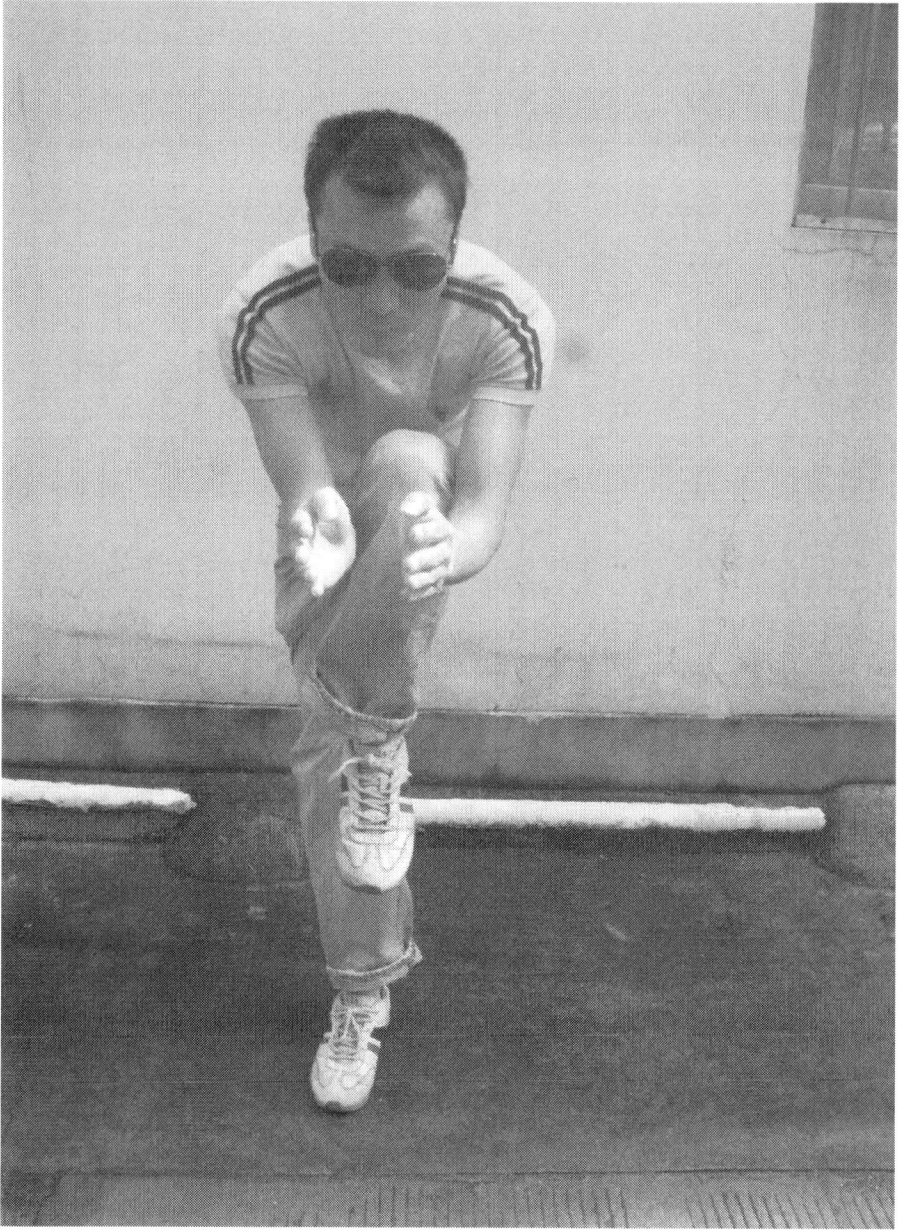

FIGURE 27

Hindu Squats

Now we will consider Hindu (or Deep) Squats. This will increase the power of the kick, and help increase the height of the kick. Do this immediately after the knee raising exercise, without a pause. There is some risk in this exercise, so do it carefully, and slowly at first, trying to do it the way described.

1. Elbows are pushed forward and downwards in a double Jum Sau position, back vertical, feet pointing slightly outwards. (Figure 28). Ensure that your knees bend in the direction your feet are pointing. Doing it so that the knee bends in a direction other than the way your feet are pointing is risking damage to your knees.
2. Squat as far as you can go, being careful not to impact too hard at the bottom of the squat, or again, you can damage your knee. (Figure 29). Control the descent, especially for the first few, going slowly and getting faster with each squat.
3. Then completely straighten your knees with a snap. It should just about lift you off the floor. (Figure 30). Fully straighten the knees.
4. Repeat 20 times.

This should be done slowly for the first one, getting faster each time until you are going as fast as you can for the last half of the repetitions. This is **not** designed to strengthen thigh muscles, as most squats that people use such as in a gym, but instead are intended to increase the range of motion and power for kicks. If you simply want to strengthen thigh muscles, then only go through a small range of motion, and do not go into a deep squat – but that won't help your VTK. Doing it this way will immensely help your kicks.

Some common errors include just using the thighs instead of completely going down, bending forwards too far, only going part of the way, doing it like a thigh squat, not keeping the back as vertical as possible, moving the knees in a different direction than the feet are pointing. This last one can cause injury to the knees.

FIGURE 28

FIGURE 29

FIGURE 30

The Ten Second Walk

The Ten Second Walk is done by lifting your knees up to waist level and shaking your foot and lower leg. It might look funny, but this gets rid of toxins in the blood so that your muscles will be less likely to ache in the morning. It is a modern relaxation and recovery method added in for health, and it takes a bit of coordination to walk knees raised and shaking the calves. You just do this for about ten to thirty seconds to relieve the pressure on the students before moving onto the next exercise.

It is usually done after standing in stance a long time such as when you do a long form, or, more usually, after a lot of knee raises and squats, especially when you do 3 repetitions of the pattern described in this book.

Getting Up Exercise

This is usually done at the end of a series of floor exercises, when you are already on the floor.

This exercise is vital for complete Ving Tsun Kuen training, as it teaches how to get up off the floor while fighting, still leaving your hands free and being stable for the whole movement.

Tragically, this exercise is largely lost from Ving Tsun Kuen these days. It is, or at least was, part of the ground fighting section of Ving Tsun Kuen.

There are several ways to lead into this, as it is very difficult to learn. It is, unfortunately, the one and only part of traditional Ving Tsun Kuen that relies on a certain amount of agility flexibility and strength. It is significantly harder for those older, taller, and less flexible.

First and foremost, in developing the necessary flexibility is to go to the floor in reverse of how you get up. When you go to the floor, you should hit the deck hard while doing this exercise in reverse, and not just slowly get down like an old man or cripple. It is important for learning how to fall as well, so the shoulders and back hit, while you keep your hands in front guarding, and not hit your head.

Because of this, we will consider the exercise from standing to getting down, then from the floor upwards. Usually this is done at least 3 times in quick succession, at least once and maybe twice during the exercises, and whenever you go to the ground, you do the downwards side of it to do so.

It is a very dynamic exercise, so some of the pictures are taken from a video of the movement, and are blurred due to this. It was hard to take step by step still photos.

We break it down into two phases, going down, and getting up. It is just as important going down. It will help with the stretch, the muscles, and importantly teaches how to not hit your head on the floor when you fall over

Going Down

1. Start from standing and bend the knees, put your hands up in Guard position. (Figure 31). Use a mat if you want to, although eventually you will need to be able to do it without a mat. Practice doing it on grass, carpet, wooden floors and so on before you do it on concrete or tiles.
2. Squat down until your bum is as close as you can get to the ground. Spread your feet a little if it helps, and turn the toes out. Do not use your hands on the ground. (Figures 32, 33).
3. Lie back and shoot your feet out and apart, ensuring the head and shoulders are off the ground. Basically, you are in the training stance but lying down. (Figure 34). For some people, this will necessitate falling down a few inches.
4. Keep your guard up, protecting yourself from an imaginary opponent. Aim for where the enemy would be.
5. This part of the exercise also teaches you how to fall down without hitting your head, keeping your hands in front so you don't break your wrists trying to control your fall, and they are up in a fighting position ready to defend you as well.

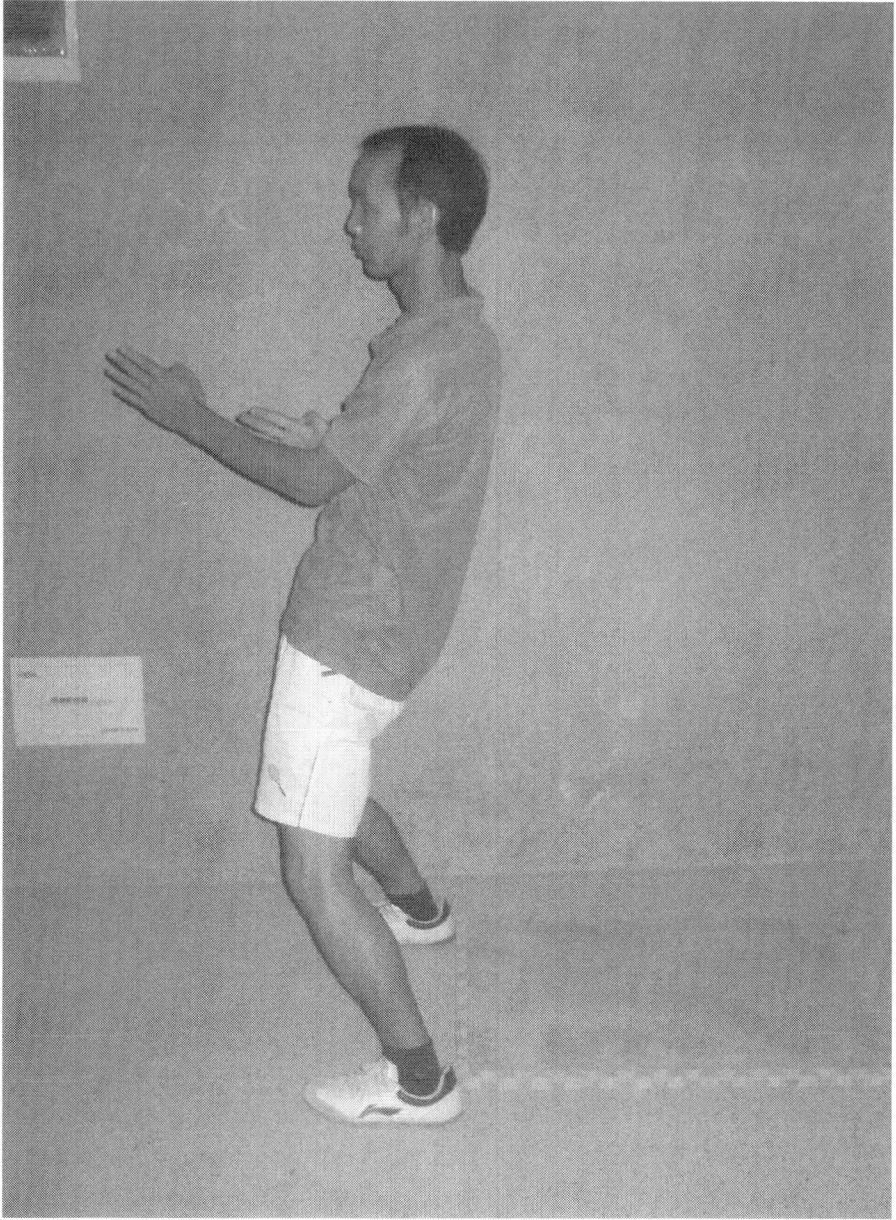

FIGURE 31

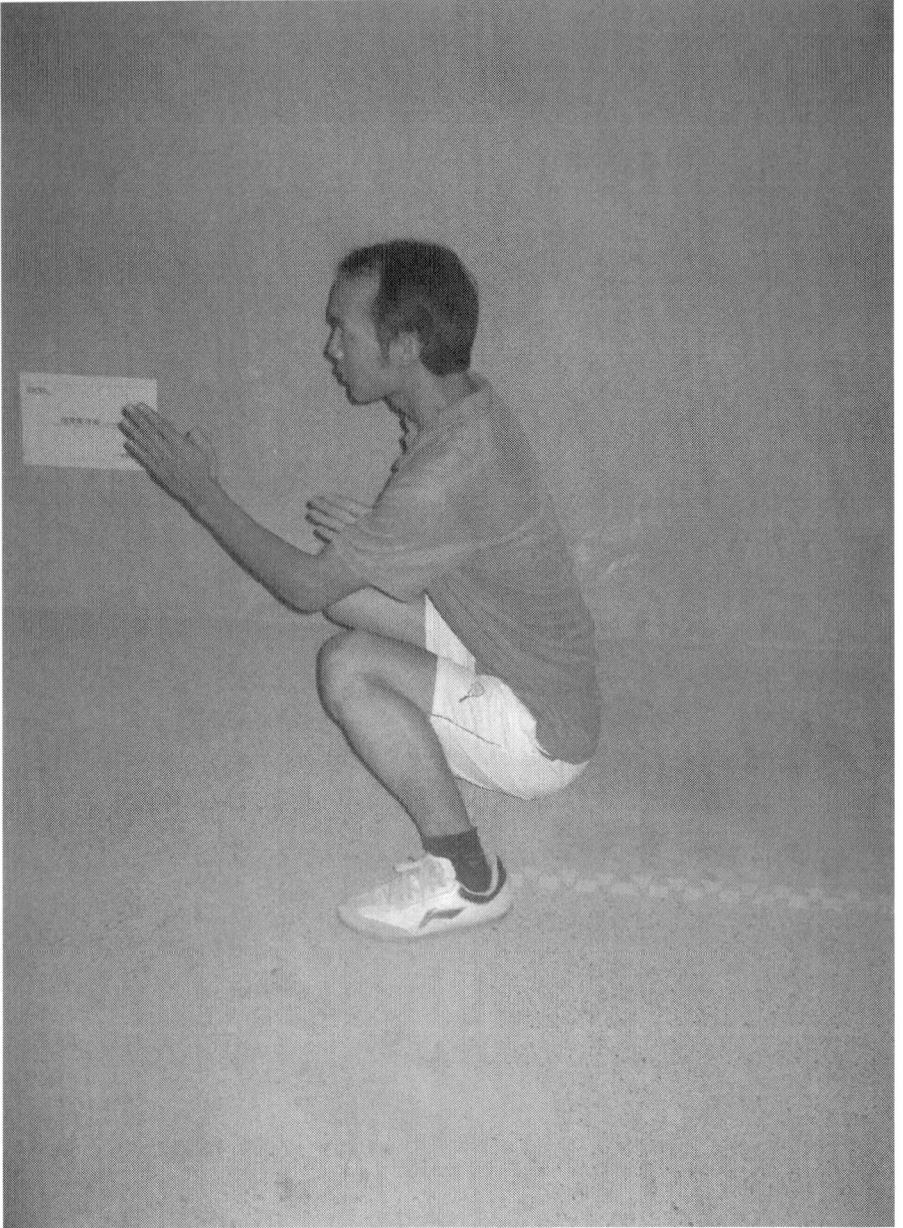

FIGURE 32

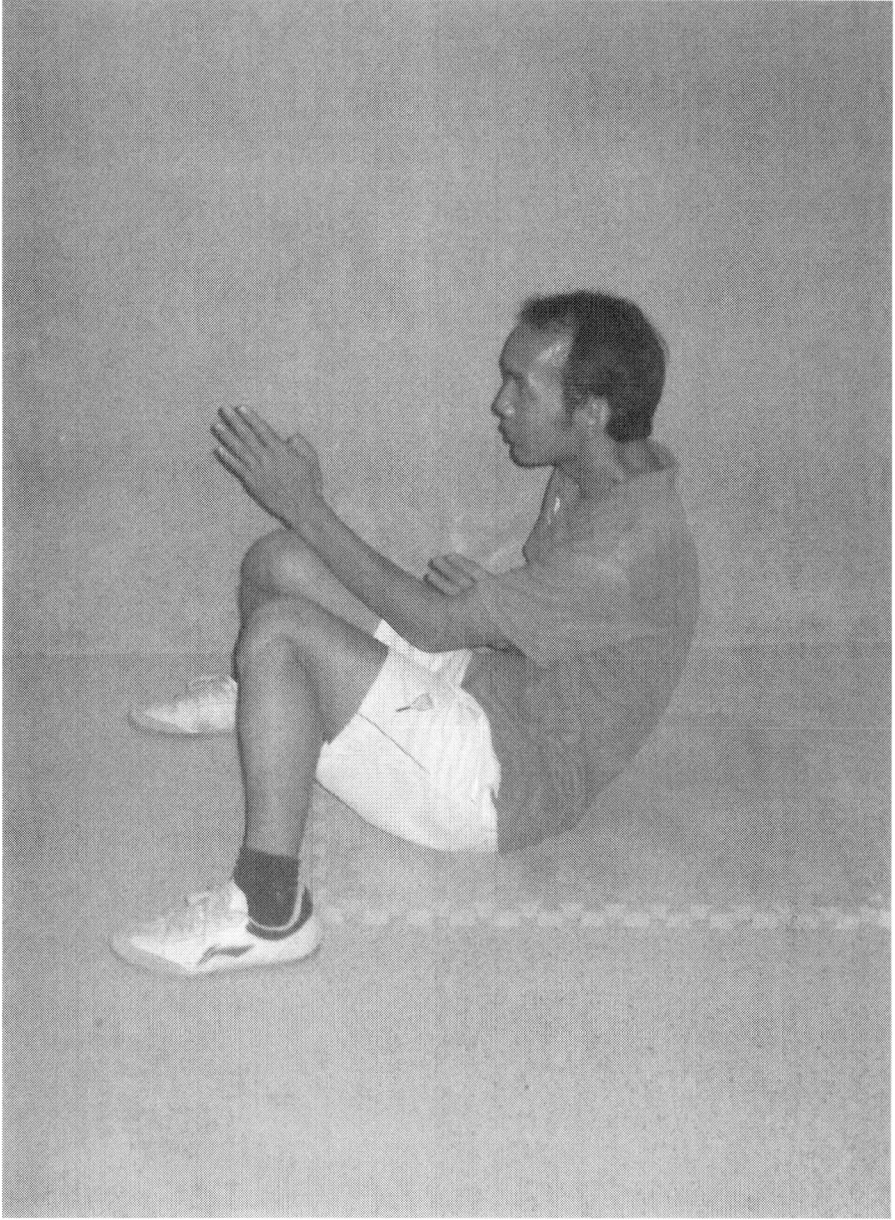

FIGURE 33

FIGURE 34

Getting Up

1. Lie prone on the floor, feet apart, hands in guard position. (Figure 35). You should be starting from where you left off the previous section of the exercise.
2. Snap your shoulders over your waist as you put your feet under your waist. If you can do this while your bum is still on the ground you have it made. If not, you will need stretching and training. (Figure 36). Sit-ups and other exercises will help.
3. Stand straight up, keeping your guard up. (Figure 37). Once you can do that you can punch as you rise.
4. Once you are standing, snap the feet into the training stance. (Figure 38).
5. For more advanced practitioners, once they can do this adequately, they can instead step forwards punching. (Figure 39). Or backwards, punching.
6. Reverse the process going back down, so you can strengthen the muscles and stretch the limbs.
7. Do it at least 3 times total in quick succession.

FIGURE 35

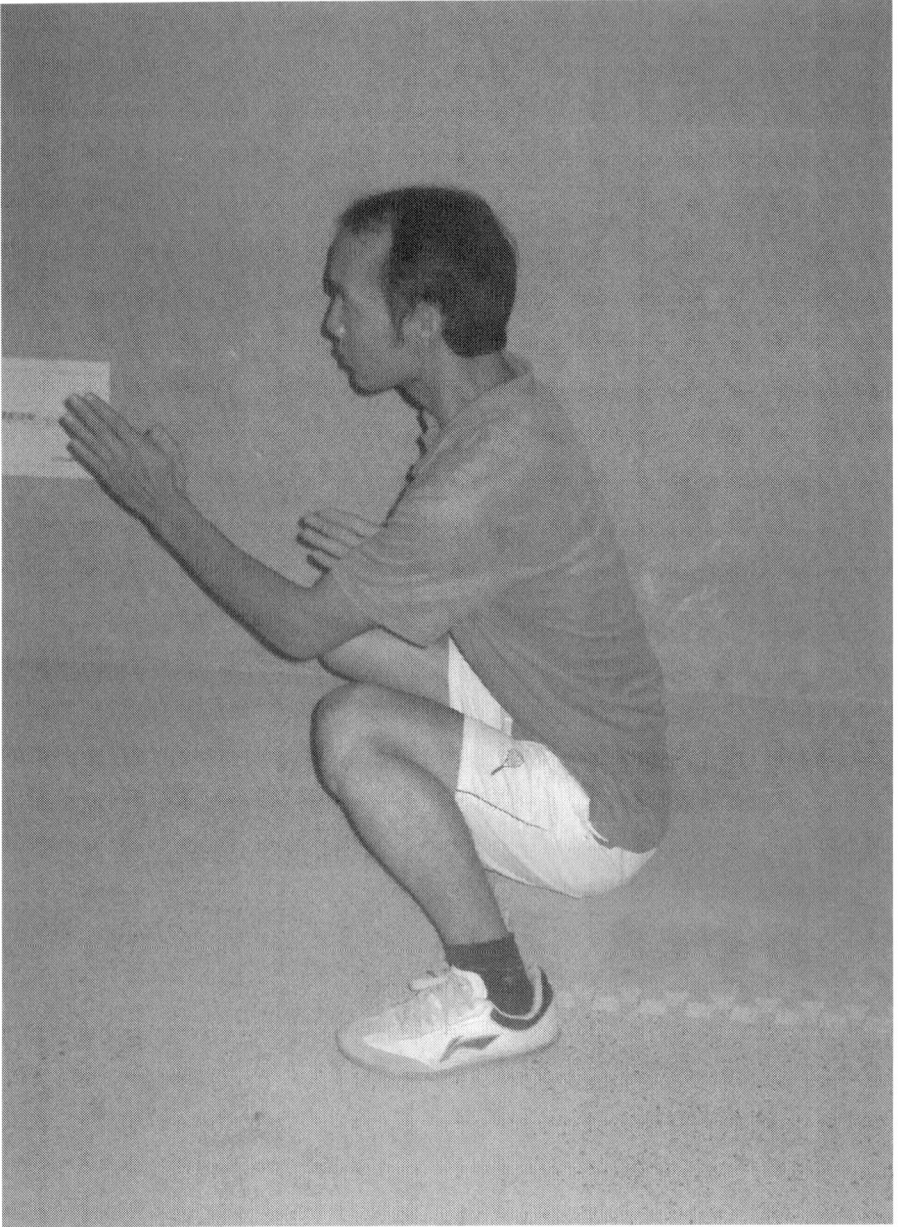

FIGURE 36

FIGURE 37

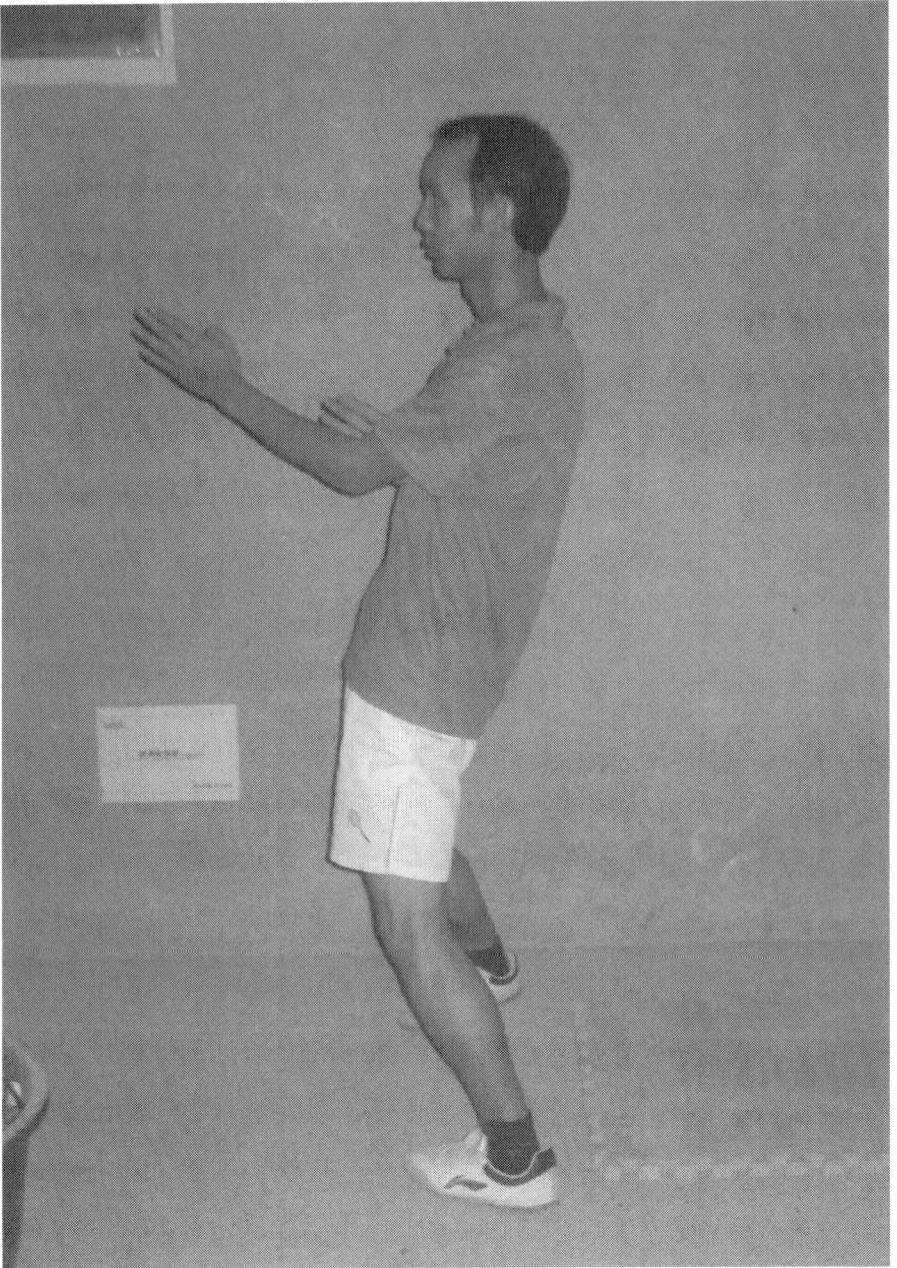

FIGURE 38

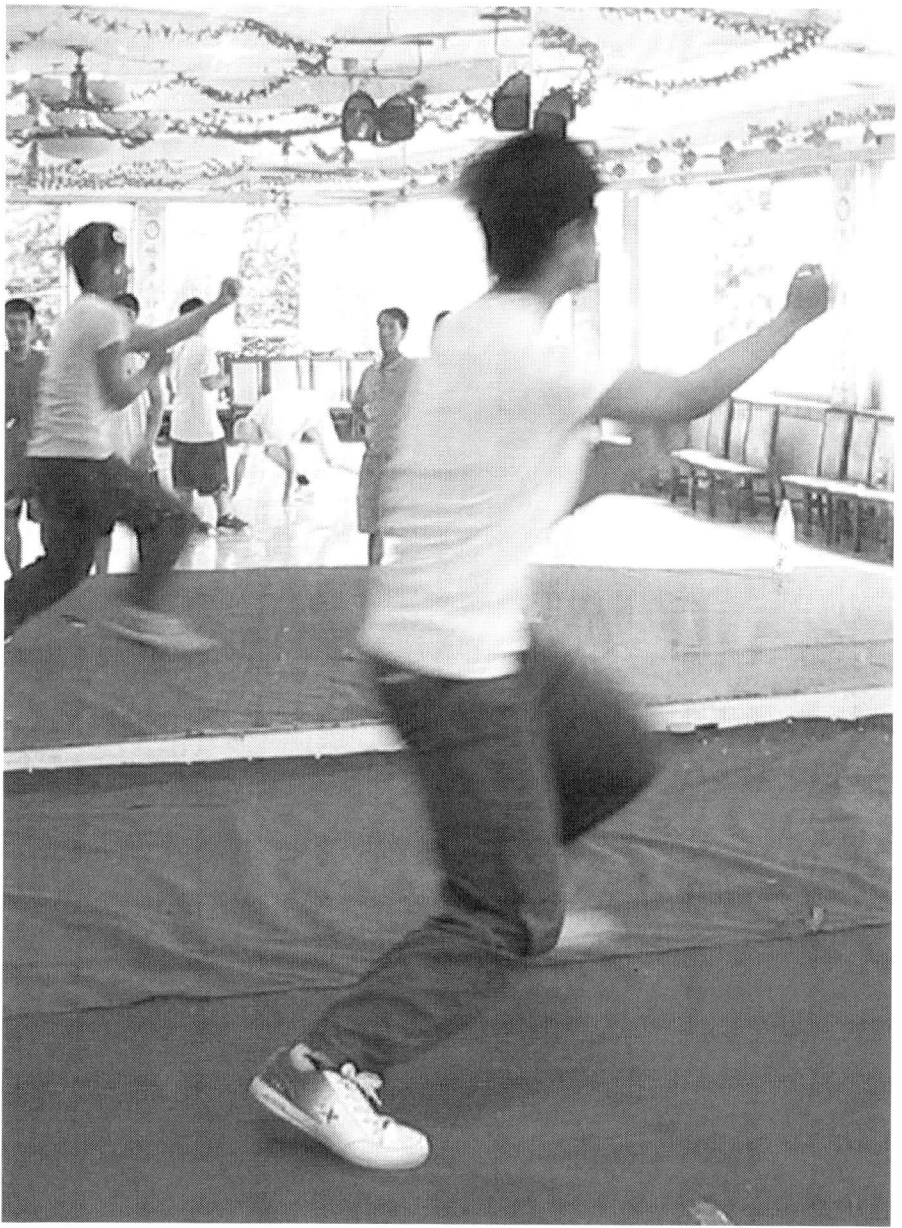

FIGURE 39

This is a difficult exercise, and may take some time with exercise and stretching to accomplish. This exercise is for when you are knocked to the ground, so learn to hit the deck without injury and get up fast. Unlike other methods of getting off the ground, it is stable throughout the entire time of getting up, and leaves your arms free for defence, and keeps you facing your enemy instead of turning around, which happens with other methods.

More advanced options: Once you can get up easily and naturally, this can be practiced from face down, on your side and so on.

If you have trouble doing this, as many do, you can use ONE hand to push off the ground if you can do it fast and snap it back into play once you are up. (Figure 40). Slap the ground to help get up, then put it back into guard. The other hand must stay in guard to defend. This is the minimum accomplishment, and everyone should at least be able to do this well. Do not use your hands going down, though, as that is learning to break your wrist as you fall. Keep your hands forwards as you go down.

One reason people find it hard is that they push up with their legs so their waist is higher than their knees. This will not work. You need to push your shoulders over your waist, which needs to be over your feet, and your knees higher than your waist. Essentially, the part of straightening up (or the first part of going down) is the same as the Deep (or Hindu) Squat.

If you can sit with your feet out by your sides, this is a great stretch for this exercise. If you can't, practice it slowly until you can.

Another stretch for this is to lie on your back, and pull your feet back until they are alongside your waist, with the feet pointing out. The knees, waist and shoulders should be also on the ground. If you can't put them all on the ground, then you hold your ankles, and using your waist, pull your knees towards the ground and over time you will get them there.

FIGURE 40

Punching

Punching is very important to any martial art, especially VTK. Therefore, a lot of punching should be done each class. There are many punching drills, but the ones listed here are more or less the kind of punching that is done as exercise, to develop the muscles for power, to develop the strength of the ligaments, tendons and joint to take the impact, and to make a fast, powerful coordination of the complete punching technique.

There are many punching drills throughout the system, training many aspects of VTK. The ones here are to learn to punch powerfully, and reflexively extend your hand through the target no matter what.

This kind of drill is done a lot at various times during class, at the end of class and after punching the wall bag as well as in the exercise program at the beginning of class. **You can never do enough punching.** After all, it is the most important technique in the whole system.

How to punch correctly and well with power is the subject of another one of my books, as it is a far too long a topic for such a short booklet, the aim of which is to get the exercise program down on paper. However, it is vital that students learn about the punch in detail, and not fudge it, wasting time and effort, and not being able to injure the enemy when the time comes to use it. I recommend purchasing my upcoming (at time of writing this) book "From the Heart" which is a full treatment on the topic of punches and follow the exercises and drills given there first, in order to get the punches correct in shape and form and movement before training them hard. Get the errors out first.

Usually we do fifty, as hard as you can. There are variations of this drill for various levels of student and for different remedial purposes in getting the technique correct, or combining it with other techniques, such as a block, or other punches.

A quick series of ideas about the punch:

1. The full cycle goes:
   a. Left hand is front guard hand. (Figure 41).
   b. Right hand punches. (Figure 42).
   c. Right hand becomes front guard. (Figure 43).
   d. Left hand punches. (Figure 44).
   e. Left hand becomes the front guard hand, (Figure 45). This is returning to the start for a full cycle. Ensure you return to guard each time before the next punch.
2. The guard has straight fingers and wrist, not curled up. Relaxed but firmly in place and pointing at the target, not in the air or to one side, or pointing over the head.
3. The punch is not a horizontal punch but a **rising punch** from solar plexus height to the shoulder height in training, or mouth height in a fight. Ving Tsun Kuen is a stand-up style, while others hunch down. Our shoulder height is around mouth height for them. Also, this is the longest punch distance, straight out. And the most powerful, with the shoulders and back and entire posture supporting it. This height helps emphasize the best aspects of the punch.
4. The punch is a straight rising line and **does not circle.**
5. The returning hand is also a straight line, deviating as little as possible other than to get out of the way of the oncoming punch. The hands lightly brush as they pass each other. Do not create a distance between them. Do not create friction between them either.
6. Leave the guard hand out until the punch crosses it. This will help control the enemy.
7. The hand doesn't clench until just before impact. Until then it is straight and in guard.
8. The wrist doesn't cock up exactly. It simply lines up with the elbow. And it only cocks up to the position ON impact not before it, or you waste your time doing it. It is to put extra energy on impact to **overcome the inertia of the enemy's body**, so the punch can continue and do more damage.

Common errors are circling the punch, making a fist too early, not making the guard part of the punch after striking, pulling back one hand too far before punching with the other one, hammering the punch, punching from face height instead of chest height, not making a fist, and being too tense.

The list of errors is too large to go into here, and I refer you to an upcoming book on the punch "From the Heart" for details.

FIGURE 41

FIGURE 42

FIGURE 43

FIGURE 44

FIGURE 45

50 Hard Punches

Traditional Ving Tsun Kuen. These are done in the normal Yee Chi Kim Yeung Ma training stance. These are usually done in the warm up at the start, and cool down at the end of class, or randomly during class before changing partners. This should be done every day at least twice, usually in the warm up and at the end of class. Other times, randomly during class. And as often as possible in your own training outside of class.

This is good for conditioning your body to knock down your opponent, by always fully straightening your arm, so that you can't pull the punch, always doing maximum damage. Make each individual punch as hard as you can. Take your time, no need to hurry.

The punching drill given here are those punches that are done during the warm up. The other methods such as for the end of the wall bag training or for the end of class are given in other sections. The wall bag training is given in the soon to be published book on the punch, "From the Heart".

The exercise here is straightforward. Simply do 50 punches in the Yee Chi Kim Yeung Ma (training) stance. Do them as hard as you can for exercise, do them correctly and slowly to practice good technique, fast for speed, and relaxed for warming down at the end of class or to reaffirm straightening the elbow in the punch after punching the wall bag, and at any other time you think of it.

1. Get into the Yee Chi Kim Yeung Ma Training Stance.
2. Starting from the left guard, punch as hard as you can with single punches. Don't try to "chain" them, but make each one complete in itself.
   a. If you do not know how to punch correctly, merely wait in the neutral position until everyone else has finished.
   b. If you are a beginner, do the punches with emphasis on the technique not power. **Get them right first.**
   c. If you know how to punch correctly, do it as hard as you can.
3. After you have finished, pull back your hands into fists at your side in the neutral position and wait for the others to finish.

50 Punches, Wide Stance

This is usually done at the end of one of the leg-stretching exercises. Essentially, this stance is simply the normal Training Stance done as wide as you can, with the feet at least two shoulder widths apart. The toes are turned in as much as possible. This is harder in this position than the normal training stance but try as much as you can. Usually, the student will not be able to turn the feet in very far if at all, because of the width of the stance, but the tension should be there the same as in the Training Stance in Siu Lim Tao. The knees are bent quite a lot and the waist is forward as much as possible. Basically, the tensions are the same as the normal stance, but it is just that the feet are pointing farther apart than usual, because the low stance makes things more difficult.

This is nothing more than doing some extreme position so that normal position is easy.

The wide stance is related somewhat to the combat version of the pole stance and the stance used with the Baat Cham Dao, and can be considered as preparation and training for these weapons.

1. Stand with your feet about two shoulder widths apart. Usually, you have moved into this position from the end of a previous exercise, such as 'elbows feet behind' or 'left leg out' exercises. Turn your toes in, bend your knees and push your waist forward hard. Pull your hands back to the side of your body, making fists in your armpits, the same as a wide version of the neutral training stance, and hold this position for 30 seconds.
2. If you have not yet learned to punch correctly, you continue to hold this position until everybody else in the class finishes their 50 hard punches.
3. Each punch is individually done, not chained, taking your time between each punch. If you have learned how to punch correctly, punch fifty times, each punch as hard as you can. (Figure 46).

Punching correctly can take some time even a couple of months, and if people punch hard without knowing how, they can injure themselves especially their elbows, which takes a long time to heal. Best to be conservative, and wait until the person can punch well, and is learning Dan Chi Sau and has memorized and can perform Siu Lim Tao adequately. Let the people who can't, simply remain in stance holding the position until everyone has finished.

This exercise, obviously, increases the power of the punch, and the stance and waist.

FIGURE 46

Punching Variety Drills

This is a series of punching drills. They can be done at any time, but I found the most efficient way is to get them to do them all together at the end of class. After the student can punch safely and has completed learning the whole form, the student can join in the class for these punching drills at the end of class. Before this, while the class is punching out, as we call it, the new student is being trained in how to do the punch correctly.

The student joins the punching drills at the end of class once they can perform the whole form on their own without prompting. These drills will teach them a whole variety of punching drills.

The Minimum.

At the very least, all the students must do this:

• Minimum of fifty very hard punches (hard as you can, each punch slow and hard and done individually, and not as a chain punch. This is done with good technique such as going through the guard. It is done in training stance, not fighting stance. You can start from a senior student, and each student can count to ten (You can use this to teach counting in Chinese – Cantonese or Putonghua – to help the students learn this, if desired.).

• Follow this with fifty light and loose punches, each punch relaxed and fast, but still making sure the elbow gets fully locked out. Also, this is in training stance. The punches can be without fully clenching the fist, but ensure they are real punches otherwise, and not simply circling the hands.

For a fast ending I get the students to do it from wherever they are standing at the end of the last section of training. For more time, get everyone in a circle, and begin the punching session.

Either way, the punching session finishes with Arm Rotations as a warm down from punching so hard and so many punches.

The Full Version.

If you have time, and the students are keen, then after the fifty hard punches but before the cool-down light and loose punches, you can perform this series of exercises: Select the appropriate ones from the list, or do them all. There is never enough punching.

Each student chooses an example exercise from this list. They stay in stance and do it from memory—the punching exercise must be continuous and they must stay in stance the whole time. Then the student announces the exercise and ten punches of the chosen type of drill are done. The next student chooses another one, and so on, until the students have chosen a type of punching drill. All are done in training stance. Most are done from guard position, except when specified. This kind of exercise exposes students to types of punching they aren't familiar with, or trains with ones they haven't done elsewhere for some time.

This is not a complete list, and you can make up your own, but even without more, this is enough for 25-30 students as is for each to do one, counting the alternating sides and multiple punches. On the other hand, it is not necessary to do them all on any one training session. You can easily get up to 500 or 1000 punches in this way.

- Doubles – first left then again with the right hand (all even numbers must be done first ten with the left hand then ten with the right hand, usually with the next student in the circle counting out the ten for the opposite hand. Odd number punches automatically even out.)
- Doubles using the front hand first. (Alternates hands automatically).
- Triples.
- Quadruples. (Ten first left then ten with the right hand leading).
- Quintuples, Sextuples, and so on.
  o Can continue up to ten punches per count, with even numbers alternating starting with left hand then the same amount starting with the right hand. (All even numbers must be done first ten with the left hand then ten with the right hand, usually with the next student in the circle counting out the ten for the opposite hand. Odd numbers of punches automatically even out as they alternate automatically.)
- High middle low—triple punch, first to head, then centre, then solar plexus or a bit lower.
- Tan Da (Alternating sides each punch).
- Tan Da using front hand to punch.
- Tan Da doubles same hand.
- Tan Da doubles opposing hands.
- Gaun Da (Alternating sides each punch).
- Gaun Da using front hand to punch.
- Guan Da doubles same hand.
- Guan Da doubles opposing hands.
- Tan Da then Gaun Da same hand.
- Jum then Punch, same hand. Alternating hands. This is done from either guard using back hand first, or from neutral training stance.
- By number up—this means on the count of one do one punch, on two count two punches, three means three punches, all the way up to ten punches.
- By number down—as above but counting down from ten, with ten punches, then nine etc.
- Form punches (just like in the form). From neutral stance, punch through centre, then wrist roll.

- Quick draw punches. Hands start by your sides; they are lifted up through guard into a punch. Can do doubles or singles. With pivoting, the nearest hand to enemy punches first.
- Many of the above can be done with pivoting once the student is up to it. Pivoting makes them very difficult and very tiring.

After the punching is finished, it is important to do the Arm Rotation exercise, in a relaxed fashion, as a cool down.

Two Steps Forward and Two Steps Back

This is traditional for Ving Tsun Kuen. It can be done to emphasize punching, or the stepping, or both as students get more advanced.

Do at least 1-2 min each side, building up to 5 minutes as fast as you can. At first, for beginners this is done slowly so they can do the techniques right, but over a few months or a year, speed is increased until they are doing it as fast as they can. This can be done at the end of class instead of part of the exercises at the start of class, as a cool down, or in the middle of the class as an endurance drill. It is an exercise that is quite hard to do well. The student first needs to know how to do simple Ving Tsun Kuen stepping, before this is even attempted, or the student will simply be confused.

You can also can use this exercise in a basic form, with just one step per punch, to teach movement, but it is also an ideal endurance exercise for speed and power.

1. Start with left foot forward fighting stance. (Figure 47).
2. Step forwards two steps with continuous multiple punches per step. (Figure 48, 49).
3. Then step backwards two steps, continuous multiple punches per step. (Figure 50, 51).
4. Make sure the students do not stop on the ends forwards or backwards.
5. Build up to 2 minutes each side with a one-minute rest.
6. Make sure the students do not 'dip' on the ends, nor rise up, no pauses.
7. Stepping should be light and fast.
8. Get the whole class to do it together and use a stopwatch. Students all do it at their own level. Some can do slowly and carefully if they are learning, others

one punch one step, others two or more others continuous punching and as fast as they can.

9. Give them a one- or two-minute break, before the students change legs and do it again. For the last 10 seconds of each side, really egg them on to maximum effort.

10. Increase the time incrementally to 2 minutes per side with a one-minute rest between.

The most important error in this exercise is that there should be no stopping on the ends of the movement, but be continuous and smooth. The student ideally should have advanced through several stages and now be continuously punching and stepping at maximum speed and power.

Remember to repeat the exercise on the other foot for the same amount of time.

FIGURE 47

FIGURE 48

FIGURE 49

FIGURE 50

FIGURE 51

It's a good exercise for fitness and movement, so you can do it at least once a week or so, or more often sometimes. We used to do it most classes. However, periodically check at a slow speed to ensure they do not lose the correct stepping positions.

First, think of it this way: In fighting stance with the left leg forwards, step forwards and punch – the left leg should still be forwards. Now step backwards – the left leg should still be forwards.

You have just entered a fight and got back out again. This is an important idea. It means that as you step in and out, you can't afford to stay in or you will get hit. In and out in one move. Smoothly.

Now you step backwards, one step, then step forwards one step. You are now stepping out of a fight then in. Again, you cannot afford to stop on the backwards move, but move out and in smoothly without pause.

Think that it is one step forwards into a fight, then immediately take one step back out. Then one step out and immediately one back in. In, out, out, in, and continue. You can't let your feet leave the ground since you are in contact range, you can't dip or plant your feet too firmly, or you will not be able to move lightly. You must instantly change direction and be under control. This is very useful and practical for fighting, and if done well and fast and hard, it will also improve endurance. Once you have done it for long enough, say 2 or 3 minutes of continuous fast smooth pace without pause, take a short rest then do it with the other leg forward as well for the same time. It should be exhausting, not done casually. Ideally, it is a way to make the students do some hard training finish off the night.

Part Three

Useful Non-Traditional Exercises

These come in a few different categories. I've divided them by usage here. Note that some are used in Ving Tsun Kuen, but different variations etc or mixed with other things, so I have grouped them here with non Ving Tsun Kuen exercises simply to save discussion on what is pure Ving Tsun Kuen and which is not. It's just the exercises, though, that have been changed. We would not change Ving Tsun Kuen itself.

Miscellaneous Exercises.

I put here two completely different exercises that have nothing to do with Asian Martial Arts at all. I wanted to put them together to get them out of the way first. They are sometimes hard to justify in a traditional sense, but they are very good in direct application to our martial art in a practical sense.

One is Jumping on the Spot; the other is Back Forward Back, which is a ballistic arm stretch.

Jumping on the Spot.

Essentially this exercise is done first at the beginning of the exercises at the start of the class, and it is very good for enabling the student to be able to move quickly in and out of combat. It has the same result as skipping rope used in boxing, but has a couple of advantages over that exercise.

Firstly, it takes less room in a class full of people, and doesn't need a rope, which in a crowded room is a minor hazard.

Secondly, the launch it gives you is greater for entering a fight from further away, and gives a broader support across the waist as you do it with your feet apart.

Sifu Barry Lee says he introduced this exercise after watching documentaries on Zulu warriors. They used to dance like this all night, then run for miles into battle with some other tribe that lived hours away, then fight, then run back home. Their endurance is phenomenal, and they are legendarily fierce in battle. Plus, it fits into our system neatly despite its peculiar origin.

It is usually done first at the beginning of exercising, and starts for about 2 minutes for beginner students, but building up to 7 minutes over time as the student gets fitter and better conditioned.

Ballistic Arm Stretches or "Back, Forward, Back".

This second one is what we call "Back, Forward, Back" and is, as far as I can find out, a Special Forces exercise and used in Ancient Greece for Pankration and not found elsewhere that I can determine. It is very good for strengthening the shoulders.

It is usually done near the end of exercising.

Planks.

These are good for core strength. We kind of have two main ones we use, one face down and one face up. Each has variations. I don't know exactly where they come from, as it could be several sources. I think mostly they are from Yoga, but Shaolin and other martial arts also use variations.

Face Down Plank.

This one is done for the core mostly for the back. The power of the elbows is also increased.

Triceps Dips.

This one is partly for the core, but more for the triceps and the waist.

Sprints.

We do sprints outside of class mostly, but we do Stepping sprints and various other types to speed up our movements, trying to cover as much distance as fast as we can. Often the techniques get messy but the object is to move fast and far.

Jumping on the Spot

This exercises is done for 2 minutes for beginners to start with, 3-5 minutes is normal training, and should build up to 7 minutes over time.

1. Start from a relaxed stance with your feet one shoulder width apart. (Figure 52).
2. Spring from the balls of the feet rather than lope from the knees, but keep your arms relaxed by your sides. This should be using your calves not your thighs, and simply springing up and down, using just the feet to launch.
3. Keep your arms relaxed and do not use them to help jump. (Figure 53).
4. If you want to increase the load on your body, you can punch while in the air. See how many you can do before landing.
5. Keep your feet apart during the time you are jumping. It is normal for them to come in. Don't let it happen. You need the wider base to strengthen the stabilizing muscles across the lower back. A narrow stance doesn't do as much.
6. You should spring **as high as you can** for the last 10 to 30 seconds.
7. Should you need to rest in the middle of the time allotted to jump, you should not simply stop and shake your feet. Instead, you should shuffle on the spot rather than stop. This will not only keep you moving but also pump the lactic acid out of the muscle and reduce the stiffness the next day.

This is good for the muscles that let you move rapidly in and out of the fight, moving lightly and fast. This is a very good exercise to start the training session. Skipping can be substituted if people know how, like the boxing exercise.

FIGURE 52

FIGURE 53

Back, Forward, Back; Cross, Behind, Cross

This is a ballistic exercise, in that you do it with as much force and speed as you can stand. This increases the ability of the shoulders to support punches and other arm techniques such as blocks. Variations of this were used by Pankration, from Ancient Greece, and it is apparently used by some modern military Special Forces. Other than that, I don't know any modern usage.

1. Standing with your feet a shoulder width apart, start with your hands straight out in front. This is just a starting position to get ready. After the first time through, you start from "2" below. (Figure 54).
2. Bring your elbows sharply behind your body with your hands still pointing forwards ("back"). (Figure 55).
3. Snap them straight again ("forwards"). (Figure 56).
4. Again, bring your elbows sharply behind your body with your hands still pointing forwards ("back"). (Figure 57).
5. Now, wrap your arms around your body, right elbow over your left, meeting at about your solar plexus ("cross"). Try to wrap your arms as far around as you can, as if trying to make the fingers touch each other across the back. (Figure 58).
6. Now unwrap your arms from your body and clap your hands behind your body, as far away from your body as you can ("behind"). Try to have your arms at least 45 degrees from the shoulder. (Figure 59).
7. Now wrap your arms around your body again, this time with your left elbow over your right elbow, meeting in the centre of your body. ("cross"). Again, trying to wrap the arms right around the back. Make sure you have the other arm on top compared to the one that is on top in point 5, (the opposite of

Figure 58 above). It changes each time. Left over right, right over left. Next cycle, if you can try right over left then left over right. (Figure 59).

8. From this position, pull your elbows back the same as in the first move, (Point 2. above, Figure 60). to start the cycle again. This is "Back" the first move of the next cycle, continue from there. (back, forward, back; cross, behind, cross.) Note that you don't do the 1 move each cycle, it's just a starting point. The only forward after the first cycle is "3". This is a point where a lot of people get mixed up for some reason.

9. Do it 20 times. Start slowly, getting faster and faster until you are moving as fast as you can for the last 10 or so, in a ballistic manner.

FIGURE 54

FIGURE 55

FIGURE 56

FIGURE 57

FIGURE 58

FIGURE 59

FIGURE 60

Face Down Plank

Variations are found in Traditional Shaolin and Yoga.

1. Lie on the floor, with your arms bent underneath you, palms on the ground facing forward.
2. Keeping your body horizontal as possible, push your elbows forward until you are off the ground, with your upper arms vertical and your elbows underneath your shoulders. Only forearms and the tips of your toes should be on the ground, your body horizontal. Hold for 30 seconds. (Figure 61).
3. Repeat 2 more times. This is good for elbow power, and for waist strength.

FIGURE 61

Triceps Dips

Variations are found in modern exercises (with a chair) and Yoga and Shaolin.

1. From a sitting position place your palms on the ground, fingers pointing towards your toes, directly under your waist. (Figure 62).
2. Lift your waist up and throw your head back, trying to put your feet flat on the ground. (Figure 63).
3. Keep your knees straight, and your waist in a straight line with your shoulders and ankles. Keeping them there, look forward to your feet.
4. Keep your waist up; bend your elbows slowly to lower your body towards the ground – but not quite reaching it – over a count of ten. It's like a backwards push up. (Figure 64).
5. Straighten your body up, throw your head back, and straighten your arms. (Figure 65).

Repeat twice more, and then shake out your arms. **This increases the power of your punch**, and ties the shoulder and triceps strength with the waist.

Finish with a tendon stretch, by leaning forwards and grabbing your feet, and holding for ten seconds. (Figure 66).

Variations.
1. Ten fast ones. This is easier, and more useful for beginners. They usually sag their waist too, so this is safer.
2. Bouncing ones – jump off the ground with them for ten jumps. **This is hard on the shoulders and is recommended only for more experienced people.** It is excellent for rapid power of the punch.

In the photos the student is not pointing his feet. The toes should be pointed. You can also cross your feet instead for extra exercise.

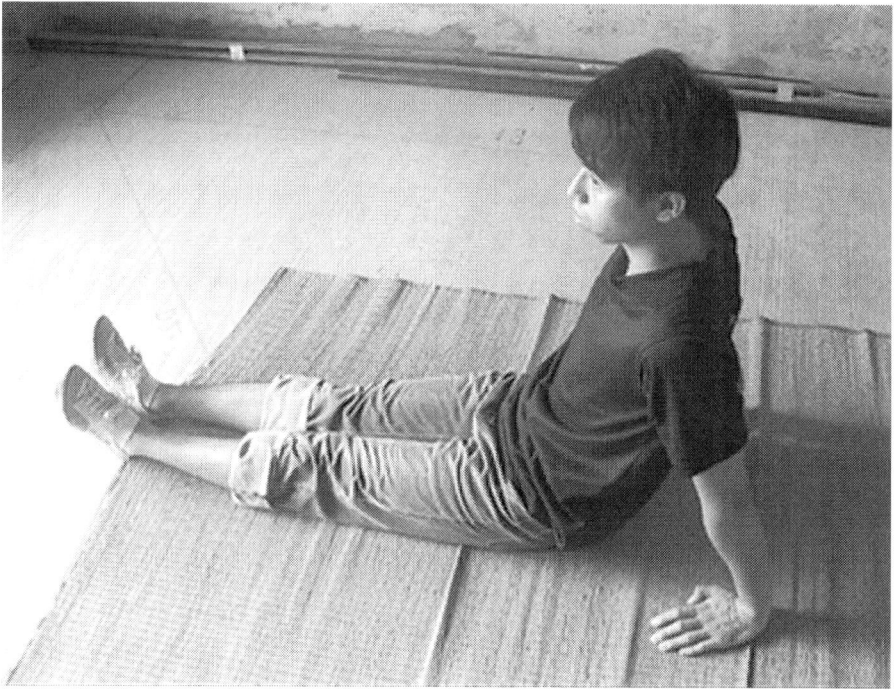

FIGURE 62

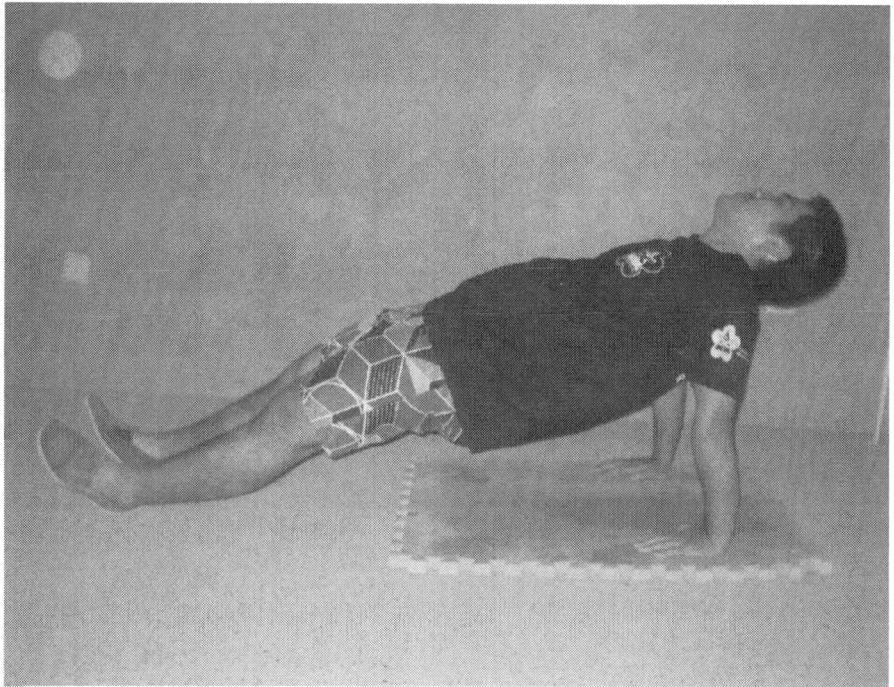

FIGURE 63

FIGURE 64

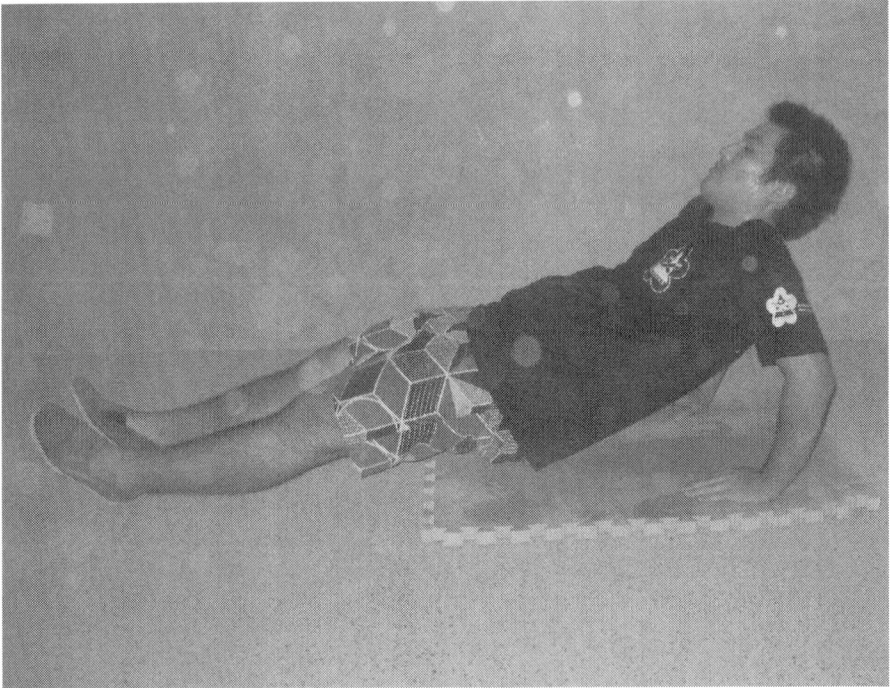

FIGURE 65

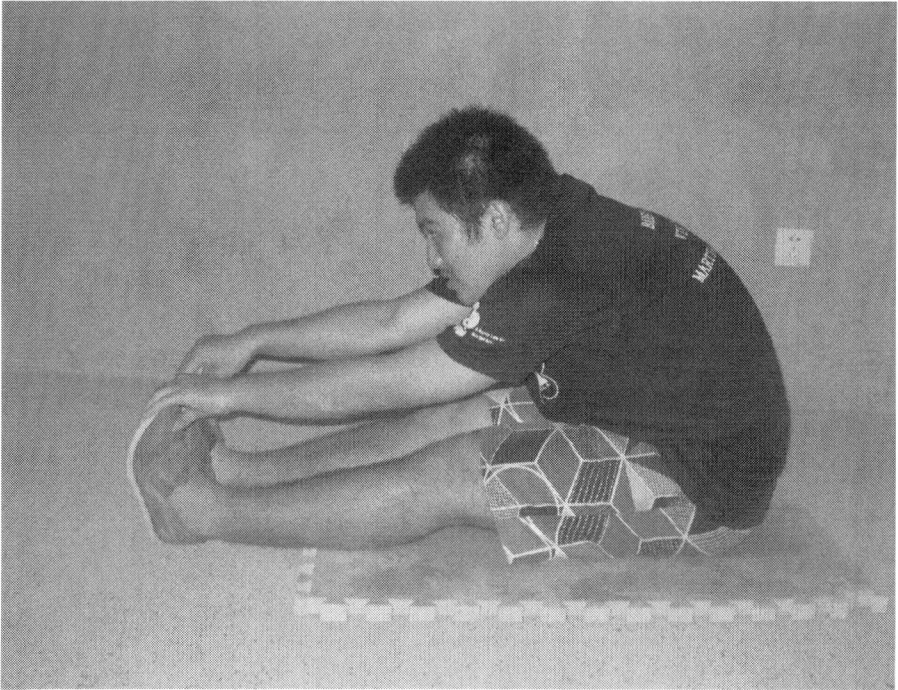

FIGURE 66

Sprints

Sprints are excellent for short term endurance such as is needed in fighting. Short sharp sprints are best, then rest until fully recovered. Some ideas are:

1. Run flat out for the length of a front fence, then walk for one or two front fences, and continue like that around the block, instead of jogging.
2. Do maximum effort stepping across the room, then rest until recovered. Note that means absolutely as much effort as possible, not reserving anything.
3. Swim across a pool the short way as fast as you can, then rest, do it again.
4. Charging across the room either with formal stepping or just crazy running, crash into walls, etc. Can include a mitt to punch into for extra training. Usually get the class to do it one after another.
5. Try 3 metres of absolute maximum crazy effort, screaming and shouting or whatever helps, then rest. Need to ensure you go completely through the 3m mark so need at least 2-3 metres after the mark to slow down, or crash into the wall. Usually need about 2-3 m to wind up to speed too.
6. Stair climbs. Sprint up a couple of flights of stairs, even just ten stairs is good. Also, you can do this as a slower, longer type of stair climb, too.

Part Four

Abdominal Exercises

I didn't put these ones in the traditional Ving Tsun Kuen section, because they have been modified from the original ones with modern ideas. However, they are essentially the same and do the same job as similar ones from Shaolin, and other Kung Fu Styles and other martial arts styles, and yes, Ving Tsun Kuen.

Drop onto your back for these exercises. Dropping down should be done hard and fast, and through the method used in reverse of the "Getting Up" exercise. Again, preparing you for hitting the floor without hitting your head or breaking your wrists.

In all the floor exercises, your head and shoulders should always remain off the ground for the whole exercise, even when waiting or taking a break. All of them increase the power and stability of the waist, useful for all your Ving Tsun Kuen. Most provide additional benefits, mostly tying your upper and lower body together, enabling you to use more of your body for power (muscle recruitment).

These are obviously good for the abdomen and the muscles used for pivoting and holding the body as a unit. They are used in every martial art in one way or another. I don't think they are traditional to Ving Tsun Kuen specifically, but there is no doubt that these kinds of exercises are vital to all martial arts training from boxing to Shaolin to Tae Kwon Do to Jiu Jitsu. Many Ving Tsun Kuen schools do them as well.

We do many different ones, but basically use two important ones, **the 'crunch' and the 'boxing' twisting type.** The other ones are for more advanced training, for longer sessions, and to mix up from being bored with doing the same ones over and over.

Crunches

Traditional Ving Tsun Kuen to Western Boxing and Shaolin and modern exercises systems.

At no time should your shoulders or head touch the ground.

1. Soles flat to the floor, bend your knees until the thighs and calves are at 45 degrees to the ground. Put your hands flat on your thighs. (Figure 67).
2. Reach up with your hands until they touch the other side of your kneecaps, using the muscles of your stomach. (Figure 68).
3. Repeat 50 times. Move directly to boxing crunches. This increases the power and stability of the waist, essential for all Ving Tsun Kuen.
4. Finish either by going straight into the next exercise, usually boxing crunches, or by stretching out your legs by grabbing onto your toes, or at least ankles, and stretching your legs until everyone in the class has finished. (Figure 69).
5. A more advanced version is to bend the elbows so they run up the thighs.

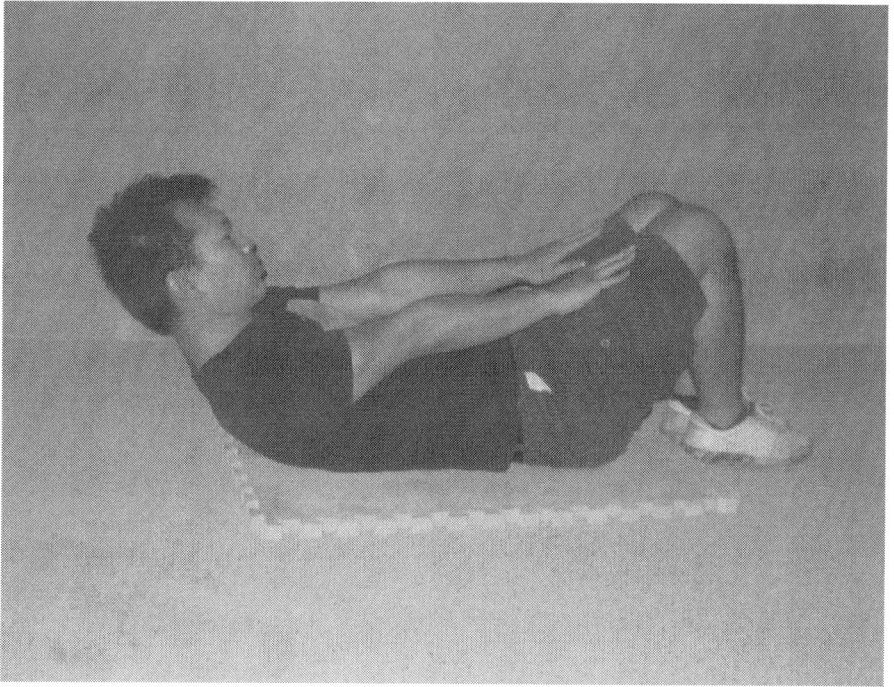

FIGURE 67

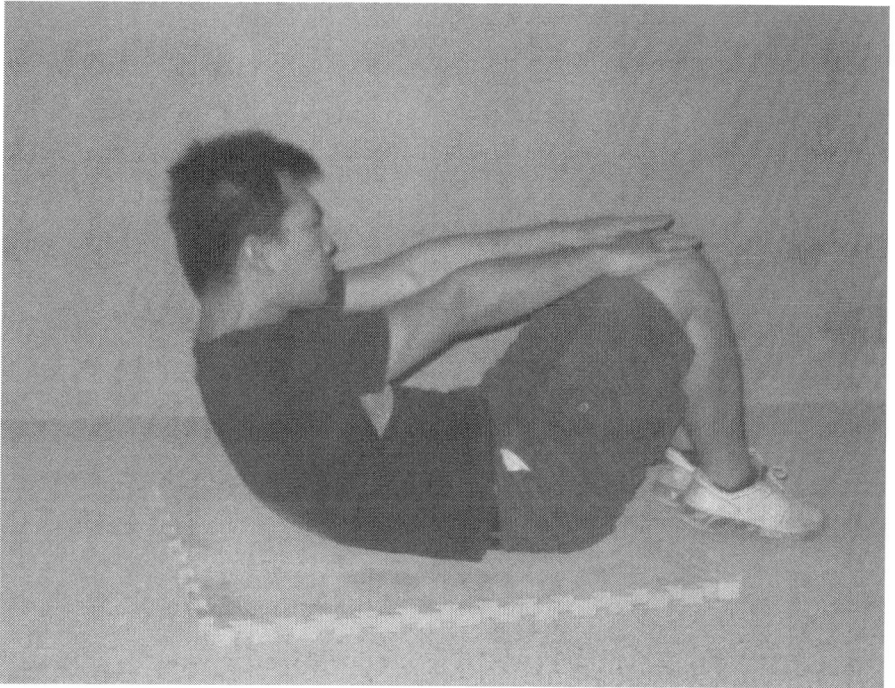

FIGURE 68

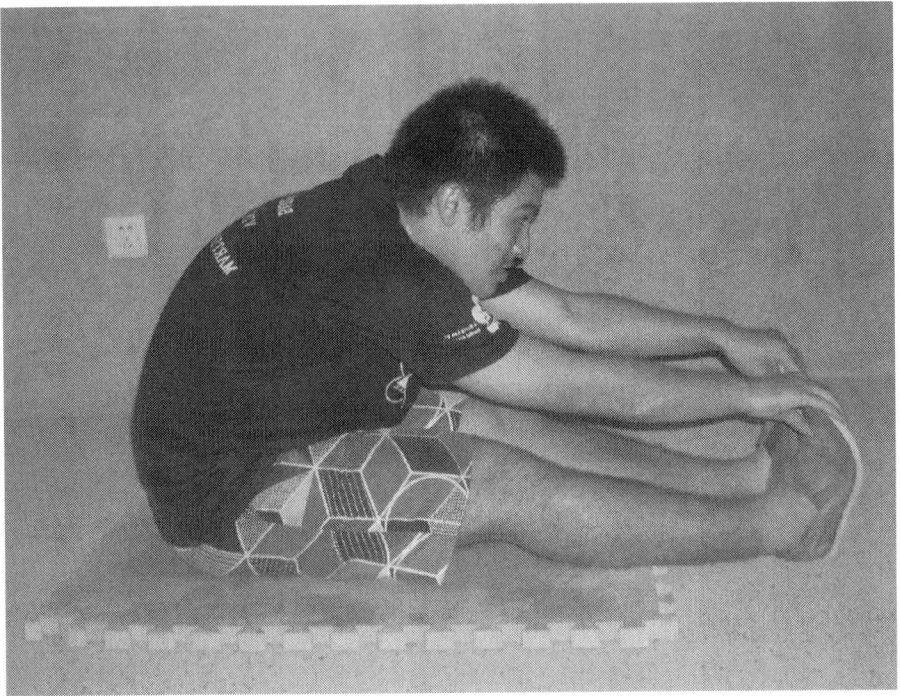

FIGURE 69

Variations:

1. "Rowing a Boat" sit-ups. This exercise is the same as for sit-ups, except your arms are straight out from your shoulders. Without changing position of your arms, do sit-ups as above. As above, but also increasing the stability of the shoulders and arms for punches etc while moving.

2. Slow Crunch.
   a. Lie on your back, arms on shoulders crossed and spread your legs to about a shoulder width apart. Keep your legs straight and point your toes.
   b. Keeping your legs apart, do half a sit up, up to the most difficult position, and stay there for 30 seconds. Do it 3 times. This exercise builds waist power.

3. Half Crunches/Flutters: In the position used above, come up slowly until it hurts at the balance point. Now, go back and forwards for about an inch either side of that position, point ten times. This should be so hard that you can't breathe properly. This is very powerful for increasing waist strength, and is a modern variation of a traditional exercise.

Boxing Crunches

Obviously, from boxing, but variations exist in many systems, traditional and modern.

At no time should your shoulders or head touch the ground.

1. Place the feet flat on the ground with the thighs and calves both at 45 degrees to the floor. (Figure 70).
2. Place your hands on opposite shoulders, and keep your elbows pressed against the body. Alternatively, put your hands lightly on your head, but this encourages people to flail around or hold the head, so I prefer the elbows tight in. Trying not to flail around, you pike up onto your bum, bending your legs. You can either leave your legs on the ground (Figure 71), or keep the legs up so only your bum is on the ground. If your legs are off the ground you will need to bring your knees closer to your chest for balance.
3. Once up, turn your shoulders to bring your right shoulder towards your left knee. (Figure 72). If you are doing the advanced version, keep knees and feet together and not moving around.
4. Then turn left shoulder to right knee. (Figure 73). Ensure you are not just using your arms or shoulders to reach the knee, but turning the waist. The movement should be very snappy and rapid.
5. Return to square. (Figure 74). You must neither come up off the ground directly to the knees, nor go directly from the knees to the ground. Ensure you come up square before you turn, and return to square before you descend again.
6. Go back down to the starting position. If you are lifting the legs up you will also need to extend them back out again. (Figure 75). The advanced version, you will have to move your knees back away from your chest for balance. Keep your calves parallel to the ground.
7. Come up square. As in point 3 above.

8. Turn the opposite way – right shoulder to left knee, then left shoulder to right knee. Snap-snap.
9. Come up square, then go back down.
10. Repeat the whole process until you have done at least 20, that is, 10 on each side.
11. Finish by stretching out your legs by grabbing onto your toes, or at least ankles, and stretching your legs until everyone in the class has finished. (Figure 76).

This will increase the power of the waist, which is needed for all your Ving Tsun Kuen, but additionally the rotation of the waist, useful for pivoting and manoeuvrability in close infighting. Boxers use this exercise a lot, with great success.

The idea of keeping your head and shoulders off the ground at all times has to do with learning to fall without hitting your head. It makes a habit of being on the ground in the correct manner. It is very important. It is part of training for 'Ground Fighting' and is also a better exercise when done this way.

FIGURE 70

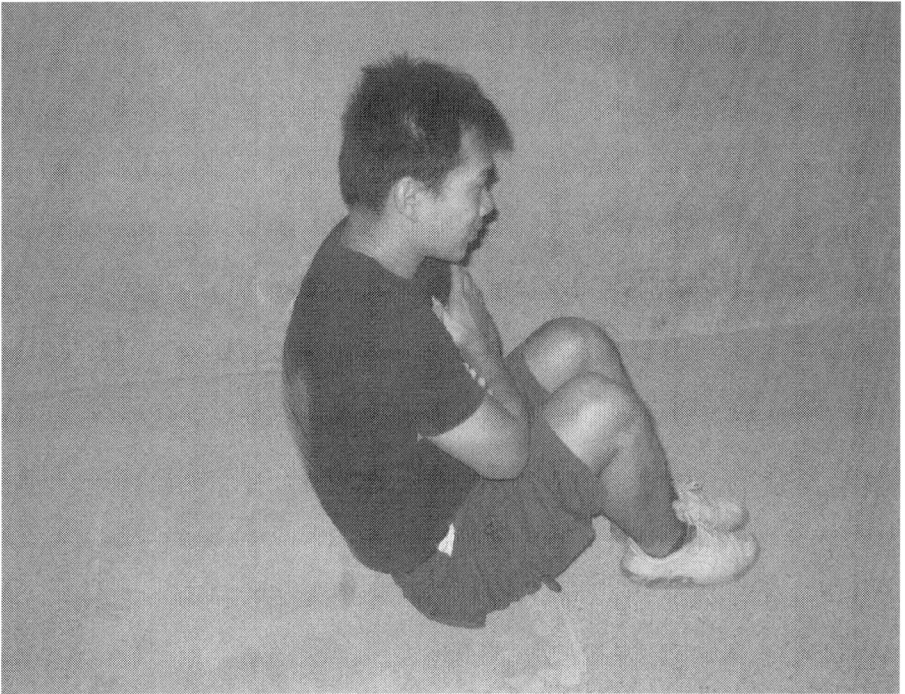

FIGURE 71

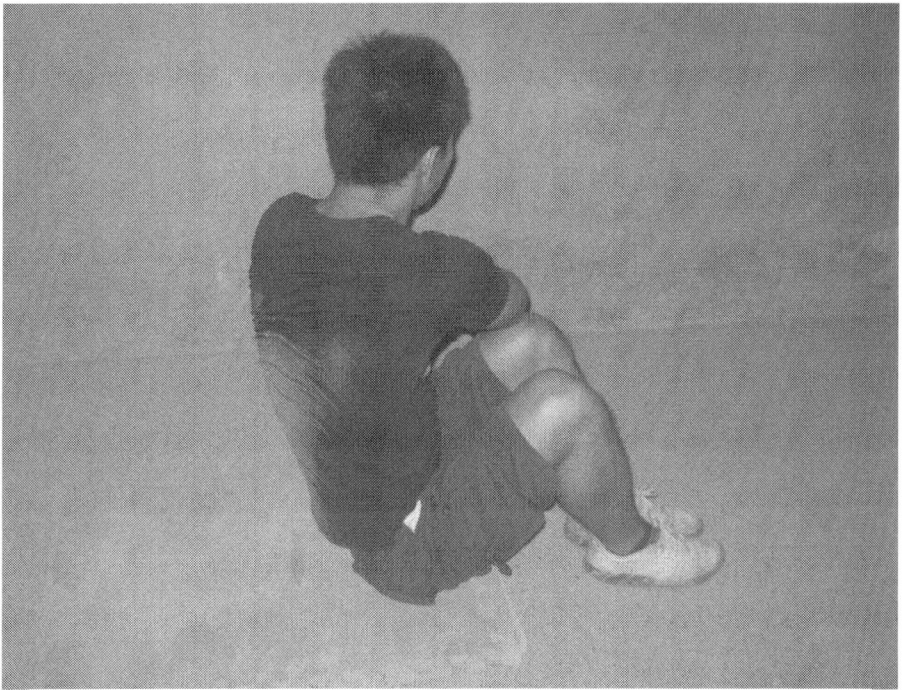

FIGURE 72

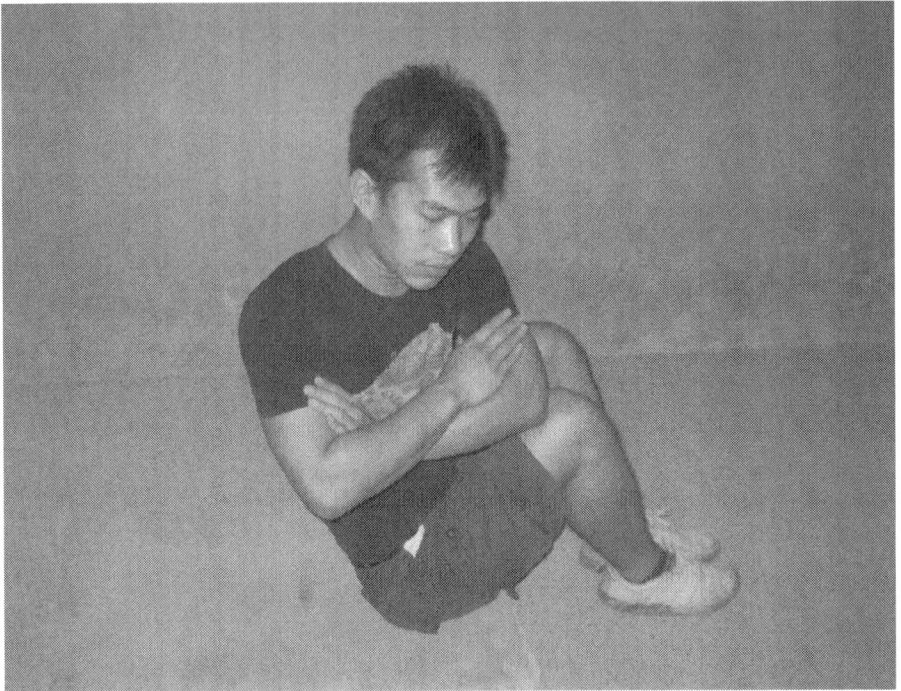

FIGURE 73

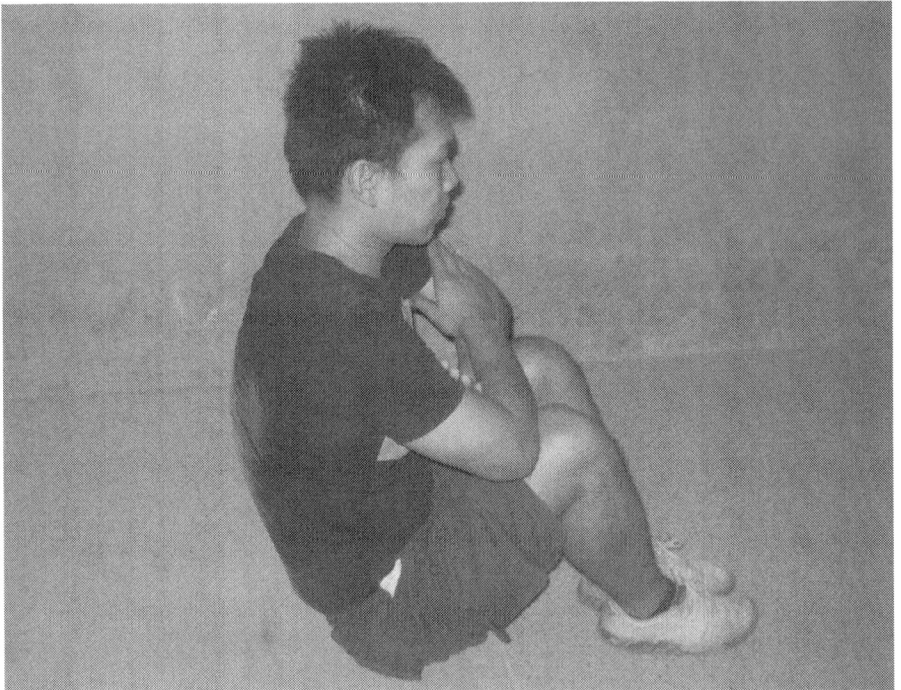

FIGURE 74

122

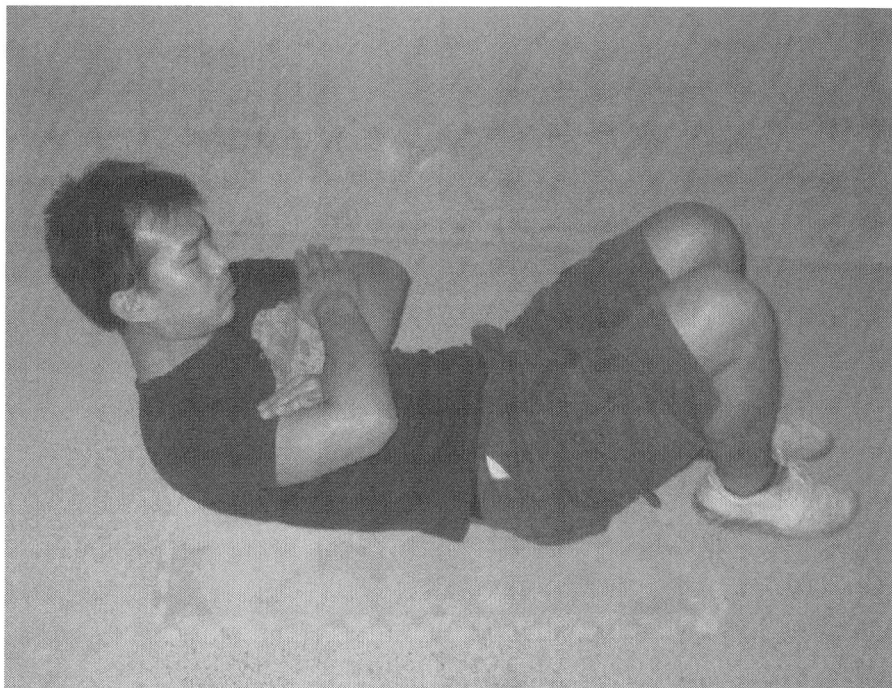

FIGURE 75

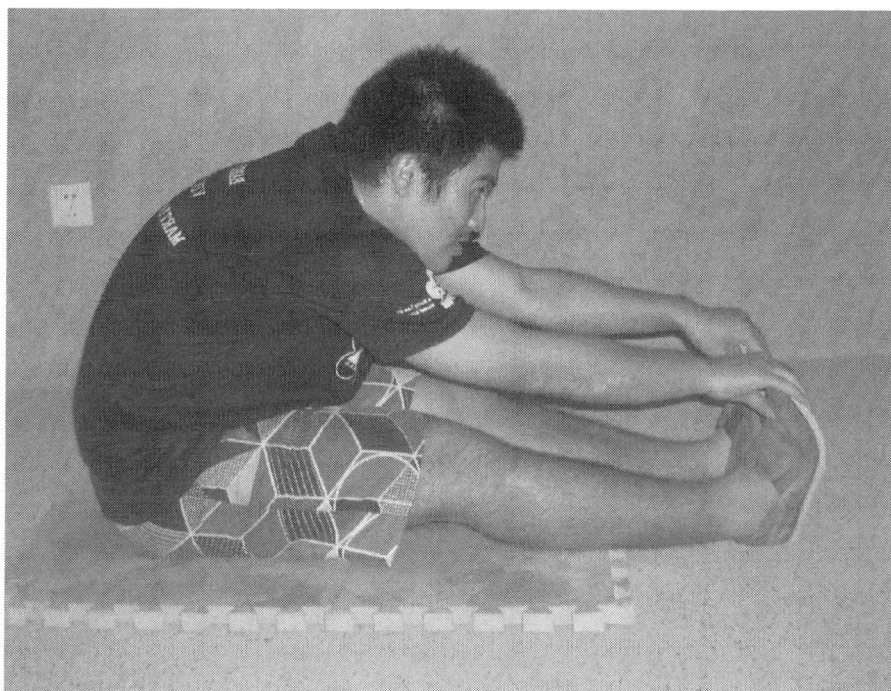

FIGURE 76

123

Variations:

Include keeping your legs in the air. For this one, ensure that you don't flail around, but control the legs so they are stable and stationary in the air. This is difficult, but very good exercise. See the pictures (Figures 72 to 77) following.

Keep your head and shoulders off the ground at all times during the exercise. Try to keep your feet from touching the ground as well, until it is over.

1. Keep your feet together, lift your legs until your calves are parallel to the floor, and off the ground level with your knees. Your thighs should be 45 degrees to the ground. (Figure 77).
2. Pike up on your bum, keeping your feet and legs in the same place, without flailing around. (Figure 78).
3. Now snap quickly, right-left, or vice versa, just reverse each time. (Figures 80 and 81).
4. Straighten up where you are, still piked. (Figure 82).
5. Lower your torso back to the ground, always keeping head and shoulders off the ground. (Figure 83).
6. Repeat the whole process, but this time turn the other way first, left-right, and so on
7. Do 20 repetitions.
8. Finish by stretching out your legs by grabbing onto your toes, or at least ankles, and stretching your legs until everyone in the class has finished. (Figure 76).

During the exercise keep your feet and legs stable and in the same place throughout, and never let your head or shoulders touch the ground.

This version is very good for control of core as well as for abdominal strength.

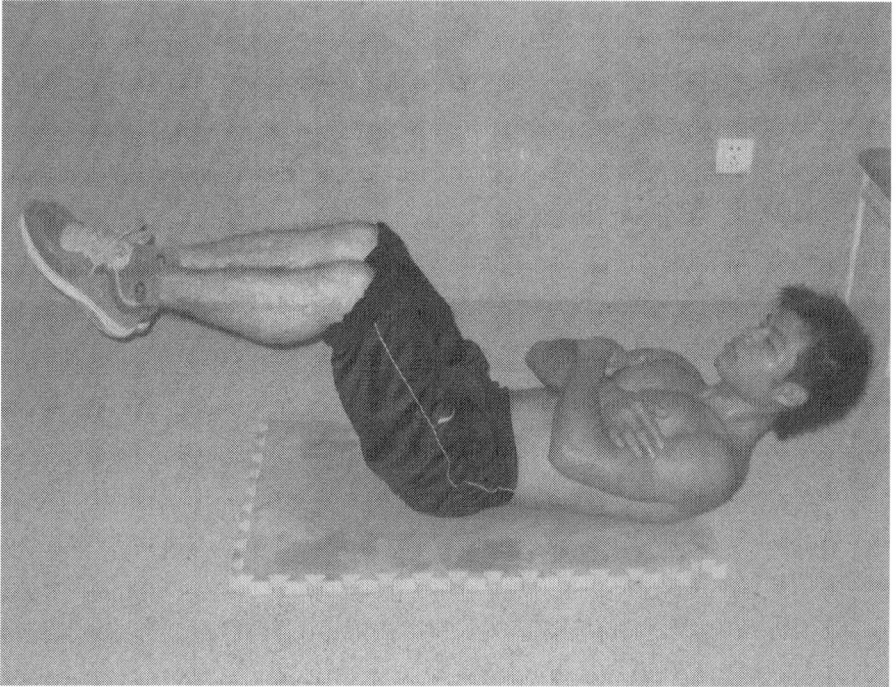

FIGURE 77

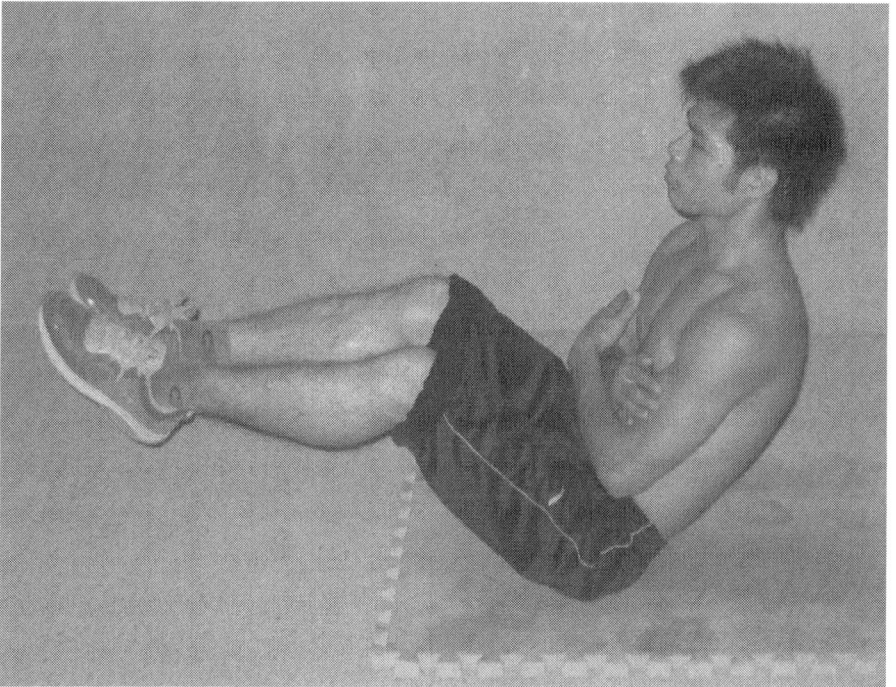

FIGURE 78

125

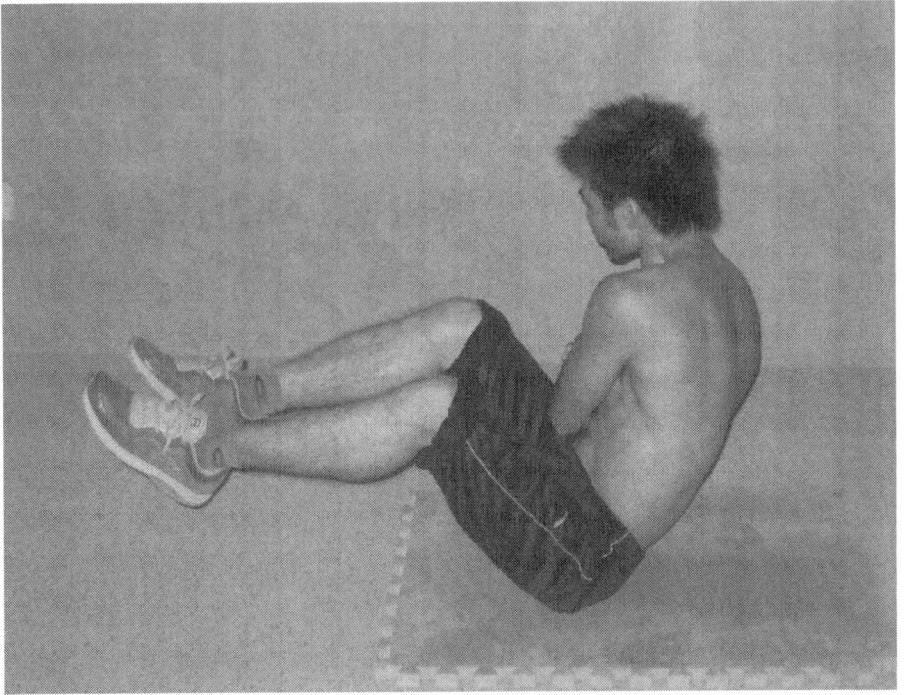

FIGURE 80

FIGURE 81

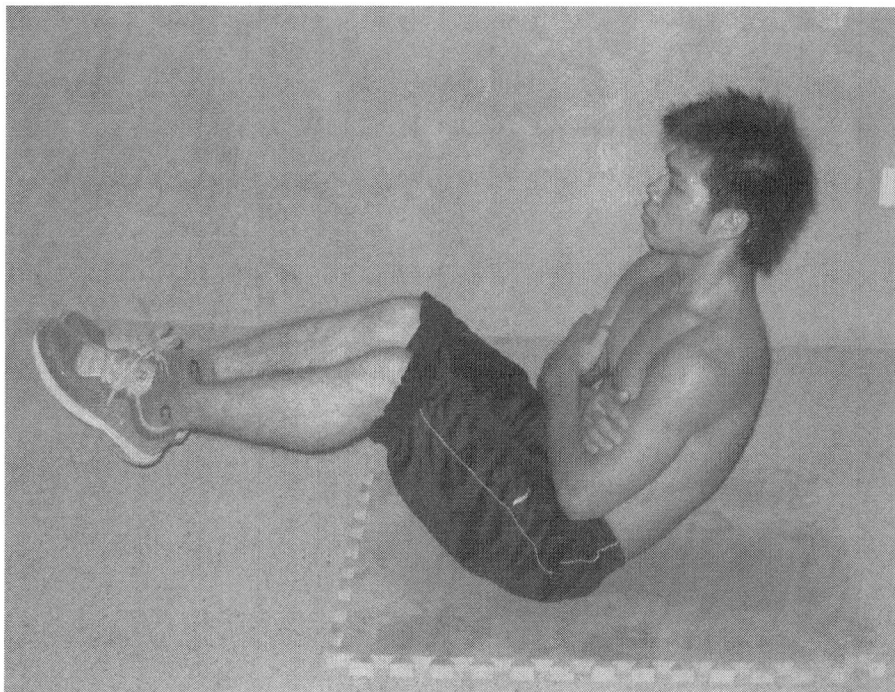

FIGURE 82

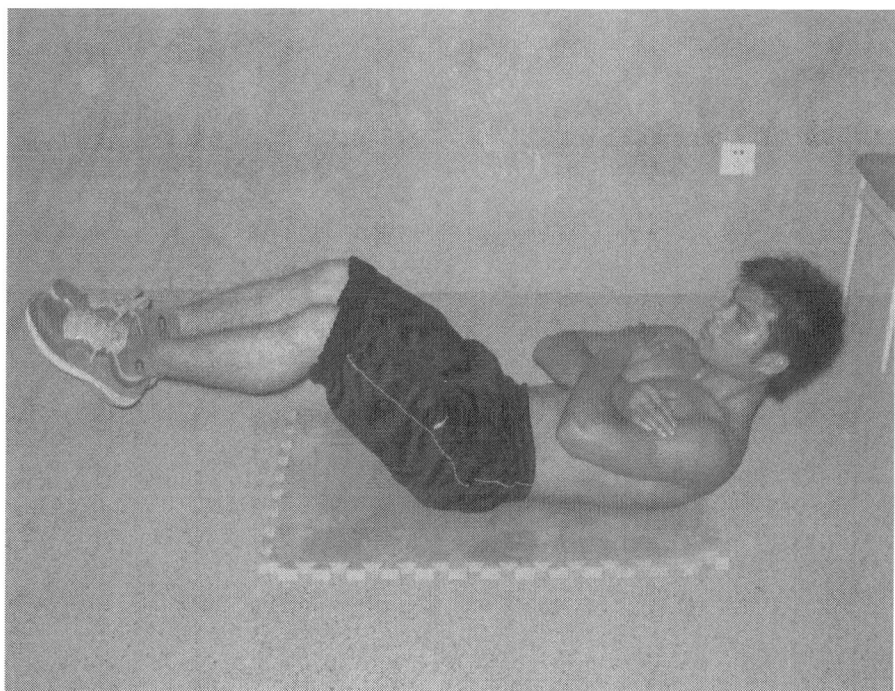

FIGURE 83

127

Slow Leg Lifts

Traditional Yoga and Hindu wrestlers, and Shaolin.

Keep your head and shoulders off the ground at all times during the exercise. Try to keep your feet from touching the ground as well, until it is over.

1. Starting on your back, put your hands in a diamond shape under your tailbone to protect it.
2. Then, lift your head and shoulders off the ground a little. Keep the head and shoulders off the ground the whole time. Your legs should be straight out in front of you and together, toes pointed.
3. Slowly (Slowly means take the time you can count to ten) lift your legs off the ground about 3 inches or so. Hold for a count of ten. This is where the exercise cycles from, so when you get back to this position, you start from here, and do not drop your legs. Keep toes pointed. (Figure 85).
4. Now bend your knees until your thighs and calves are both 45 degrees to the ground and your feet are still close to the ground but not touching it. Your heels stay close to the ground and move horizontally, and stay the same distance from the ground that they were in point 3 above, while the knees bend up into position. Keep toes pointed. (Figure 86).
5. Now, without moving your thighs, keeping them at 45 degrees, slowly lift your calves until they are parallel to the ground. Keep toes pointed. (Figure 87).
6. Now slowly raise your legs and straighten your knees until your legs are vertical over your waist. Toes pointed up. (Figure 88).
7. Now push your waist upwards for a count of ten. Point toes at ceiling. (Figure 89).

Now that you are half way through, you must reverse the whole process:

8. Slowly drop the waist until the hips are on the ground (same as position "6" above. (Figure 88).
9. Slowly lower your legs until the thighs are 45 degrees and your calves parallel to the ground. (same as position "5". (Figure 87).
10. Then, hold your knees where they are and drop your feet slowly to just above the ground. (same as position "4". (Figure 86).
11. Now slowly push your knees down until your whole leg is just off the ground. Same as position "3", ready to start again. (Figure 85).

You need to do at least 3 and preferably 5 of the whole sequence, and do it without your feet touching the ground, and without putting your head and shoulders on the ground. This exercise ties the upper legs to the waist for power especially when moving.

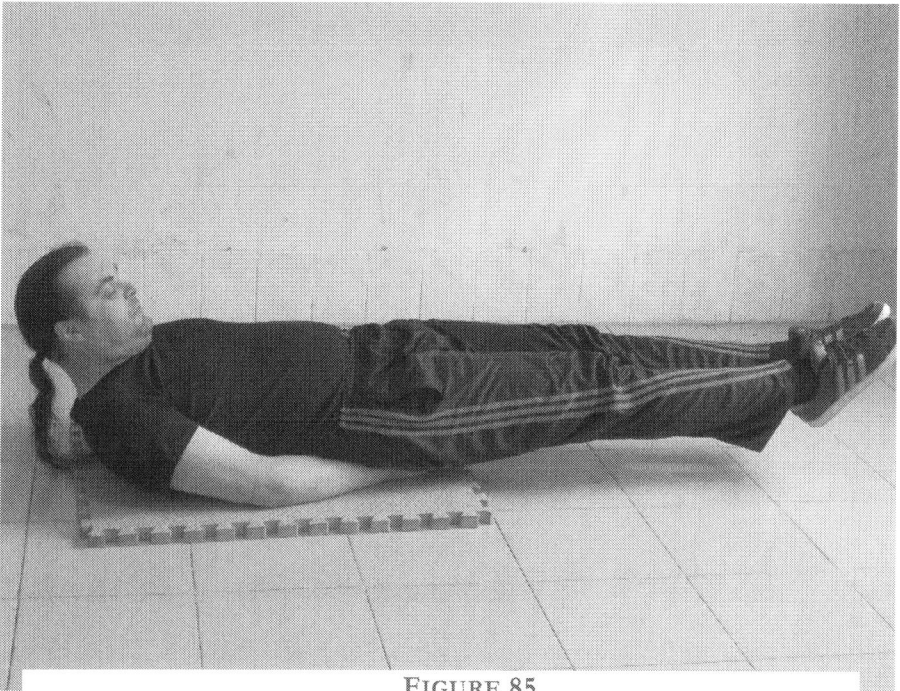

FIGURE 85

FIGURE 86

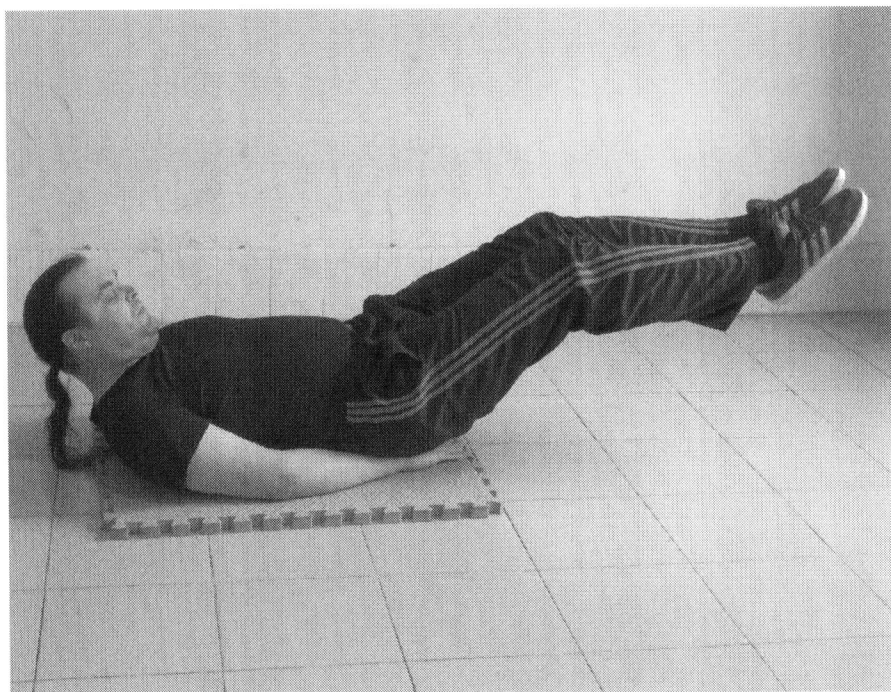

FIGURE 87

FIGURE 88

FIGURE 89

Leg Lifts

Variations in many systems, from Yoga to Modern exercises.

Keep your head and shoulders off the ground at all times during the exercise. Try to keep your feet from touching the ground as well, until it is over. In the position used above to start with (lying on your back, hands supporting tailbone), point your toes and lift legs off the ground about 2 inches and hold for 30 seconds. (Figure 90). Do this 3 times. What it strengthens is the same as above, but less dynamically, more statically – when you are standing still or unable to move. The exercise is considered risky for the lower back, so some people should do it with knees slightly bent. This reduces the risk, but also reduces the effectiveness of the exercise. Variations include lifting the legs up, bicycling the legs, or lifting them one at a time. I used to watch tv shows like this to increase long term core strength.

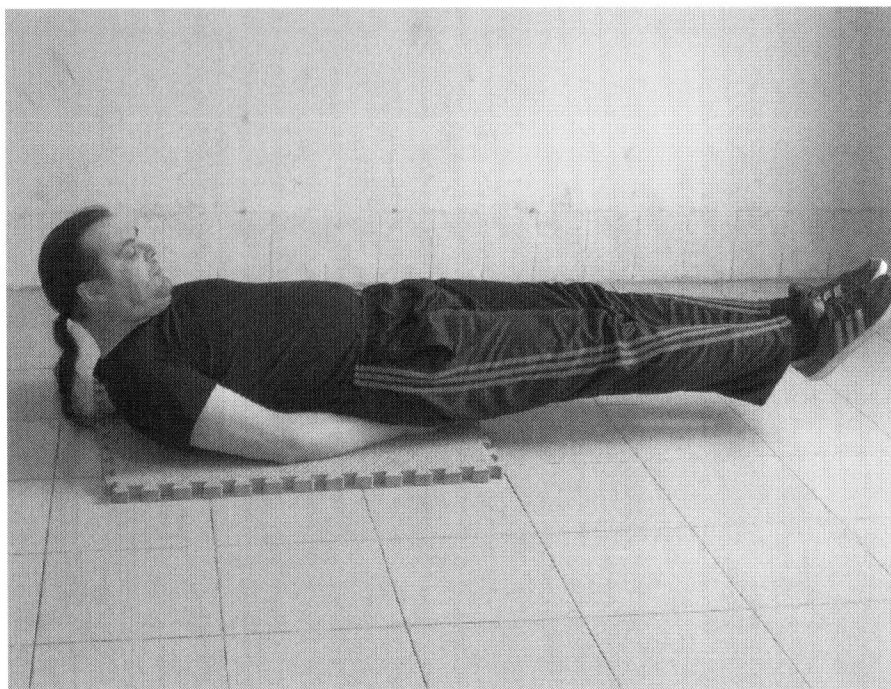

FIGURE 90

Full Sit-Ups

Every martial art has a variation of this.

Keep your head and shoulders off the ground at all times during the exercise.

1. Lie on your back. Have your feet flat on the floor, your head and shoulders off the ground. Your calves and thighs are 45 degrees to the ground. Your hands are on your shoulders and crossed (left hand on right shoulder, etc), and your elbows are tight against your body. (Figure 91).
2. Come all the way up so your shoulders reach your knees. (Figure 92).
3. Go back down until you are back in the original position. Do not let head or shoulders hit the ground.

Do 30, quite fast. Or slowly to a count of ten, do 10. This ties the upper and lower body together.

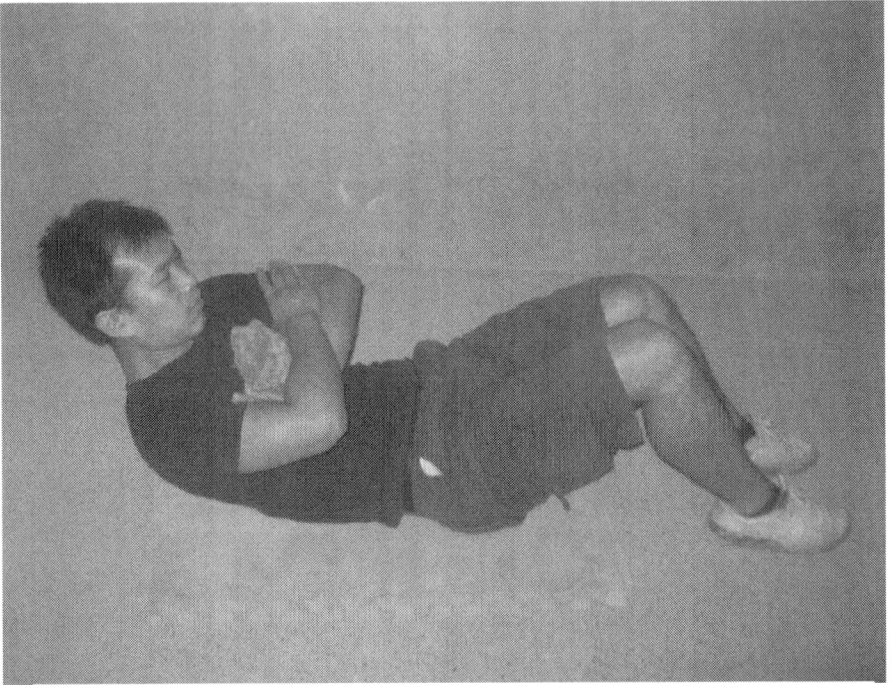

FIGURE 91

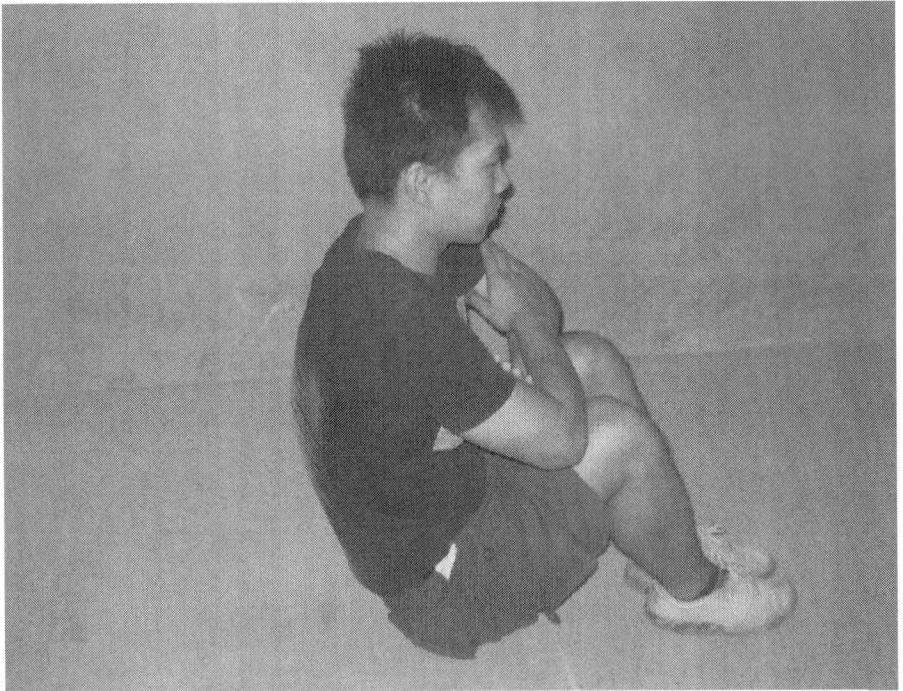

FIGURE92

136

Part Five

Yoga-based Exercises

We use several Yoga-based exercises and variations. We also use parts of Yoga in other exercise.

Yoga is somewhat ancestral to all martial arts if the oral histories have any basis in fact in that if it is true that Damo (also known as Bodhidharma, Daruma, and so on) took Martial Arts from India to China. The art Damo legendarily learned was Vajra Mushti which was the name of the warrior caste he was born into as well as the fighting system they used. This system is ancestral to modern Kalari Payat (aka Kalari or Kalarippayattu) as well as other arts from that area of the world. Kalari under that name is native to Kerala in India, and is a member of a huge and varied group of Indian martial arts dating back millennia influencing many systems throughout the region, including China, Thailand, Burma, Cambodia, Indonesia and the Philippines. Vajra Mushti is also ancestral to the various kinds of Yoga, or rather, the exercises for the martial arts side of things.

Yoga has many styles and variations, the most popular being Hatha Yoga (and its derivative forms), with another half dozen or so being well known and popular. The exercises we do are not from these ones but from a more dynamic system used by Hindu wrestlers and Martial Artists, more like the ones used in Kalari. **The one we are doing here is somewhat different from the most common forms known in the West, in that it is faster and more ballistic and physical and less about spiritual stretching and meditation.** I have had people tell me what we do is wrong. I have pointed out there was many kinds of Yoga, and that they only know one type from one family of Yoga styles, and what they are doing is not the same one. They usually not aware that there are variations. Well, there are. This is one. It might be more obscure due to the popularity of Hatha types, but it is just as legitimate, and more useful to us as martial artists.

We do several Yoga based exercises.

Greet the Morning or the Sun Asana.

We use a lot of variations as well as the simple one. I have added emphasis on the squat part of the movement for Westerners because this is difficult for us.

Reaching for the Sky.

This exercise and the 'Chin to the Knees' has been added at the end of many of the other exercises.

Chin to the Knees.

Lunges.

Praying Hands.

The Superman.

I've forgotten the real name of this, and use the one I was taught to call it by a chiropractor who trained with us.

The Bridge.

The Plough.

We used to do the plough, but I took it out as too risky for beginners. For those that choose otherwise, the only difference between the normal plough and ours is that we try to keep as much of the back as we can on the ground, and not rest it on the shoulders and neck. Emphasis is on the waist bending, not the back and especially not the neck.

Other Flexibility Exercises.

Various waist bending exercises, prone and standing, that are in this book could have been included in this section, but I have put them in other categories based on their function.

Sun Asanas

Also called "Greet the Sun" or "Greet the Morning" or "The Cobra" plus "Downward Dog", and many other names.

This is a slightly altered version of a famous Yoga exercise. Ours is modified from the Hindu wrestler's version and not the more well-known Hatha Yoga exercise, so it has noticeable differences. Ours is designed for more ballistic use.

1. Stand at attention with your feet together.
2. Press upwards and slightly backwards with your hands, stretch up, reaching for the sky. (Figure 93).
3. Bend down and grab your ankles with your knees straight, nose pointed to the ground and pull your chin towards your knees. (Figure 94).
4. Reach towards the ground with the heels of your palms. If you can, put your hands flat on the floor. If you can't, reach for the ground with the heels of your palms, and not your pointed fingers. Keep your wrists bent at 90 degrees. (Figure 95).
5. Put your palms on the ground if they are not already there. Bend your knees if you must at this point, but it is better if they are straight.
6. Put your left leg back until you are reaching back as far as you can, with your left knee is just off the ground, you are looking forwards to the opposite wall, and your waist is as low as you can get it. (Figure 96).
7. Leaving your left leg where it is, stretch your right leg back with it, so they are both back. Both are on the tips of the toes, and not the balls of the feet, if you can. (Figure 97).

FIGURE 93

FIGURE 94

FIGURE 95

FIGURE 96

FIGURE 97

8. Leaving your hands and feet where they are, now rock back on your heels, making your body into an inverted "V" at about 90°, heels to the ground if possible, and keeping your elbows straight, trying to put your forehead towards the ground, stretching calves and shoulders. You should have a straight line from your hips to your hands, with shoulders and elbows in a line, and from your hips through your knees, which should be straight, to your heels, and the heels should be on the ground if possible. (Figure 98). Now, breathing out for the whole move, bend your elbows, and touch your forehead lightly to the floor. (Figure 99).

9. Now continue moving until your nose is touching the floor. (Figure 100).

10. Now continue moving until your chin is touching the floor. (Figure 101).

11. Now continue moving until your chest is touching the floor. (Not shown).

12. Then straighten your arms with your knees just off the ground. The idea is to push up from close to the ground. Nothing should be touching the ground except the tips of your toes and your palms. If this is difficult, or for people who are overweight or have bad backs, they can put the knees on the ground for safety. (Figure 102).

13. Note these 5 moves, (Figures 9 to 13XXXX). The student must bend through this series, and end up in the position in points "11" and "12" (Figures 100 and 101) above with very bent arms and close to the ground. By the time they get to "13" (Figure 102), an unfit student will keep their arms too straight and drop their waist instead. **This can result in back injury.** Be aware of the risk of this exercise. Instead, for those that are having trouble, get them to lie on the ground, and push up into the end of the "snake" move instead. (Officially the name is the "cobra" but we use the verb "snake" when we tell people to do this section of the asana.)

14. Now lift your left foot up and put it between your palms. You are now in the reverse of the earlier position. (Figure 103).

15. Staying in a low squat, bring your right foot up. (Figure 104).

16. Leaving your hands on the ground for as long as possible, straighten your legs.

17. When your legs are straight (or your hands need to leave the ground), grab your ankles and pull your chin to your knees. (Figure 105).

18. Unlock your knees (Figure 106).

19. Straighten moving your hands vertically, then up and press slightly back into the starting position. (Figure107).

Repeat the cycle at least 3 times slowly. Usually we would do some slow and some fast, starting with slow precise ones, and ending with ballistic ones. It would be something like 5 slow, 5 variations and 5 fast ones. 3 slow ones would be considered very minimal. It is a better exercise if you do a few slow stretchy ones followed by increasingly fast ones.

FIGURE 98

FIGURE 99

FIGURE 100

FIGURE 101

FIGURE 102

FIGURE 103

FIGURE 104

FIGURE 105

FIGURE 106

FIGURE 107

There are many variations. Some examples of variations. These include:

1. Rock back then snake, rock back. Repeat it ten or twenty times.
2. After snaking forwards, snake back. This is hard to do properly. Usually it would be done after the above to end the sequence, but also sometimes 3-10 on their own.
3. Doing it with legs spread. This is more like other yoga versions.
4. One leg in the air, snake, rock back change legs, rock back, both legs back on the ground, snake, finish sequence. Repeat both sides. Reverse order for next rep.
5. One hand behind back. Repeat both sides. This is very hard.
6. After the snake, rock back, spread legs, go on toes, then first touch one knee to the ground then the other, then continue with exercise. Reverse the knee sequence for the next rep.
7. Stopping at each point in the snake, and holding for five or ten seconds.
8. Doing it as fast as possible ten times.
9. Doing it as slowly as possible, just one to three times.
10. Snaking backwards one handed each side. This is truly evil to do.

There are many other variations of this exercise, including you can also alternate left and right legs if you wish.

Deep Bends or Lunges

This exercise is done slowly.

1. Start with the feet together. (Figure 108).
2. Take a big step forwards with the left leg. Bend the front knee and come up on the toes of the back foot. Alternatively, as in the figure above, you can interlace the fingers and take the big step after stretching up and back, but this is harder to balance. (Figure 109).
3. Now, interlace the fingers, and raise them over your head, pushing up and slightly back while you bend the front knee and drop the back knee as far as you can. (Figure 110).
4. Come up to a standing position again like at the beginning, only having moved across the room one large step.
5. Starting with your other leg, do all the moves on the other side.
6. You can walk across the room like this in order to do several repetitions.

This is a good stretch for the legs, especially calves and quadriceps and shoulders.

You can vary this with putting your back foot on its side for a slightly different stretch, or putting the top of the back foot on the ground for a shin stretch.

Good for waist strength and flexibility, and ties the legs with the waist.

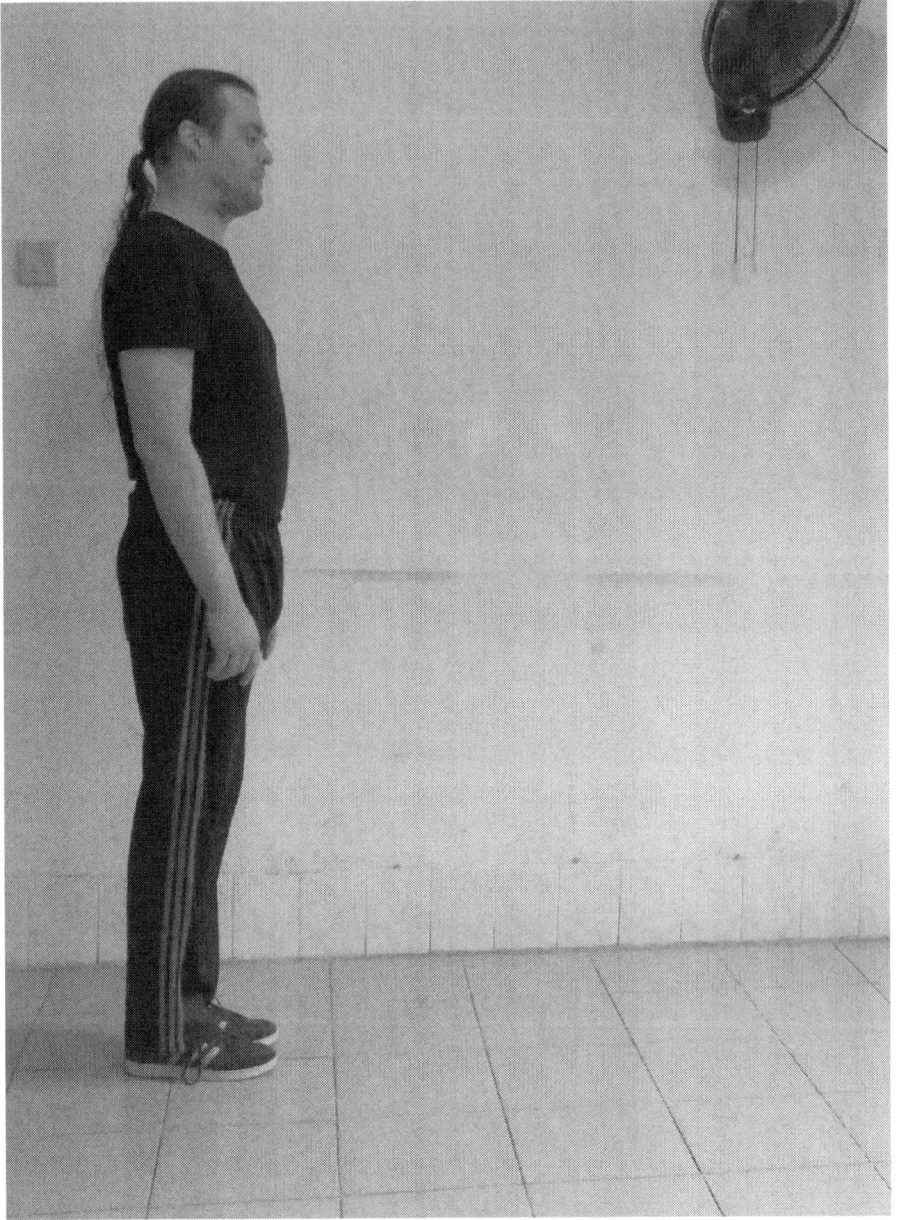

FIGURE 108

FIGURE 109

FIGURE 110

Praying Hands

In the training stance, place your palms together behind your back, with the forearms horizontal. Push your elbows back. (Figure 111). Keep your head upright and hold the whole correct posture.

Hold for 30 seconds or more.

This is a stretch to improve Bong Sau and the shoulders. It is usually done at the end of the exercises at the start of class, along with the other arm stretching.

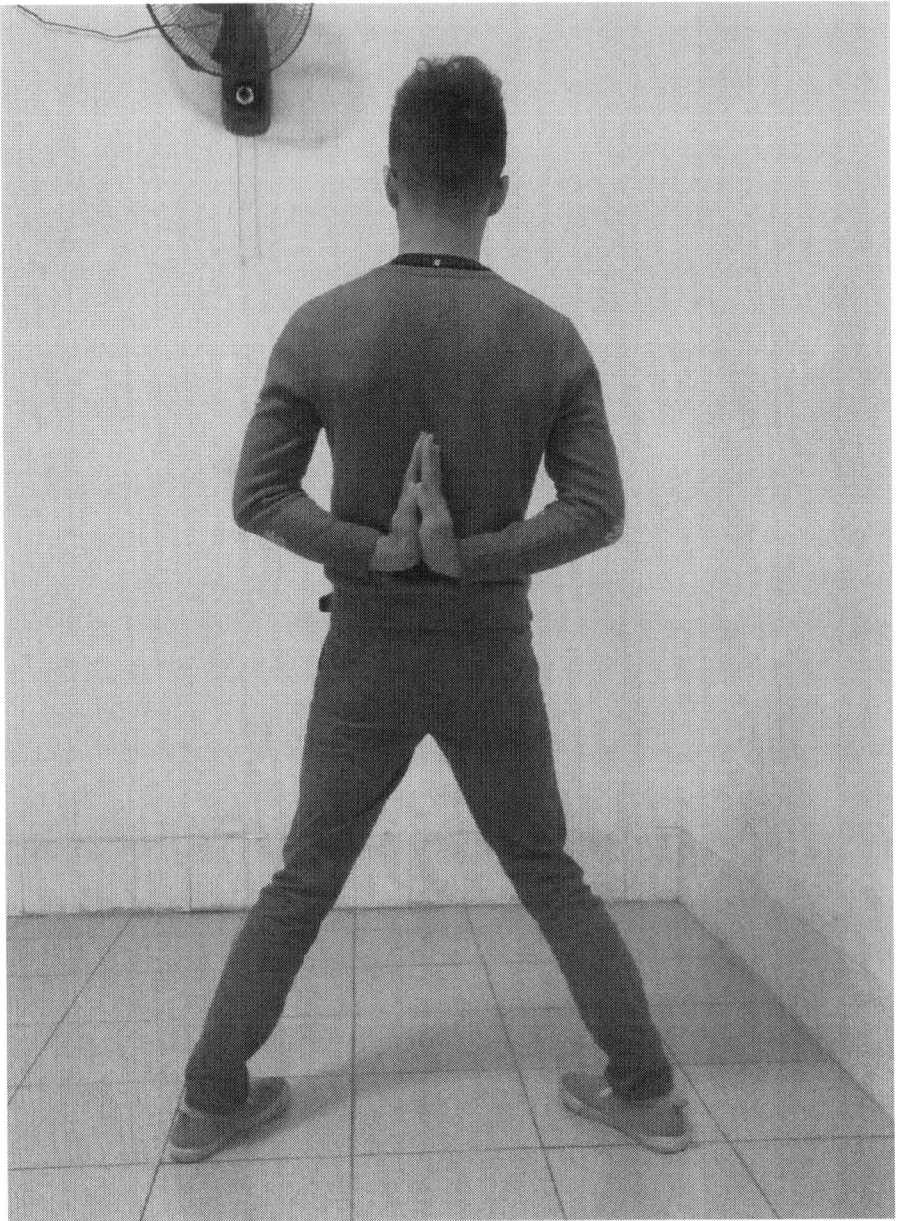

FIGURE 111

The Superman

This is a very simple exercise that stretches the back and is useful for people with certain types of back problems and injuries, postural issues and even sometimes just feels good to stretch those parts of your back.

1. Lie face down on the floor with your hands out-stretched in front of you. Your feet are together as are your hands. (Figure 112).
2. Arch your back up, lifting your hands, chest, waist, and feet from the ground, looking forwards, as if you are flying like superman. Point your toes behind you, or point them in and behind, and stretch your hands in front. Hold for 30 seconds. (Figure 113).
3. Relax and lie on the ground for a few seconds, and either repeat up to 3 times, or go onto the next exercise.

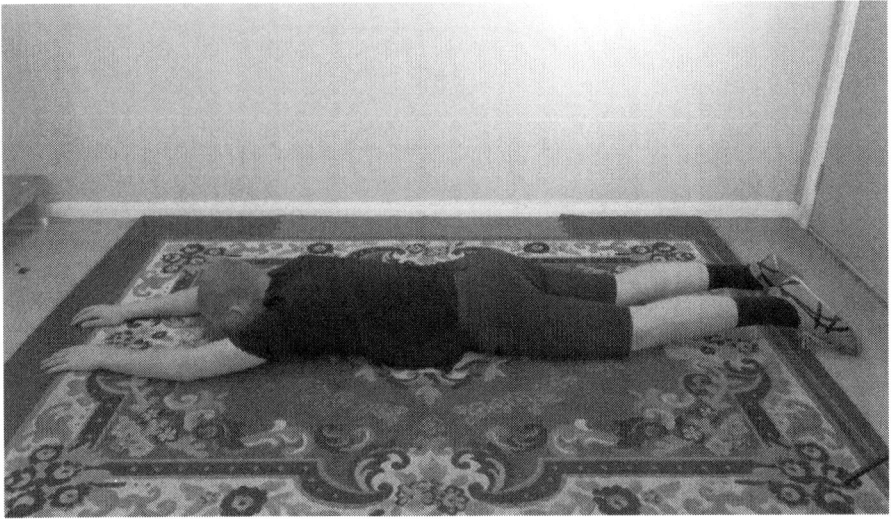

FIGURE 112

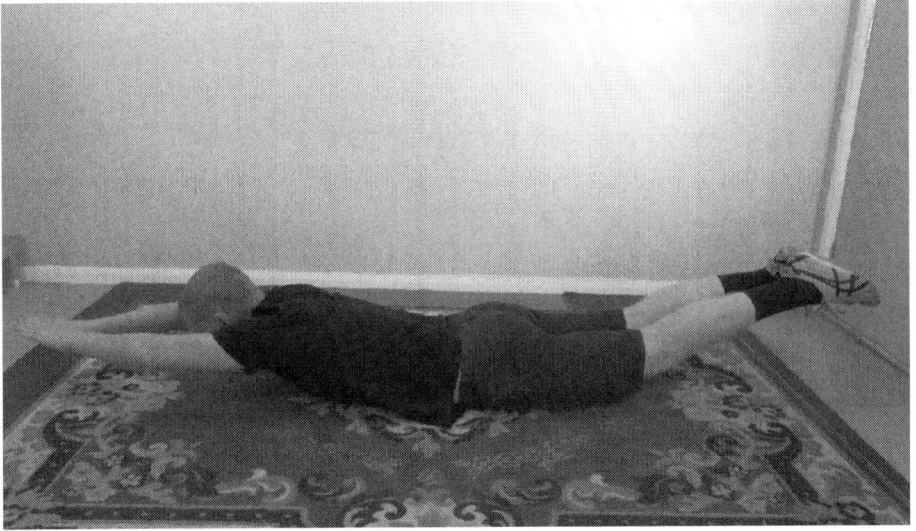

FIGURE 113

The Bridge

This is a risky and difficult exercise, but it is one of the best stretches for people who cannot do the 'Getting Up' exercise, and so I include it here. We used to do it every day, and keep trying until we could do it. It takes time, but the effort was worth it.

1. Lie flat on your back, feet apart. (Figure 114).
2. Reach up with your hands behind your head and bring your feet up (Figure 115).
3. Bridge up on the tips of your toes and fully extend your arms. Elbows straight. (Figure 116). Hold for 30 seconds.
4. Start to creep your hands and move your knees over your feet. (Figure 117).
5. Place your knees on the ground. (Figure 118).
6. Lie flat and grab your ankles with your knees, waist and back on the ground. For most people this is difficult, so pull your ankles back for a stretch. (Figure 119).
7. Hold for 30 seconds.
8. Straighten your knees and relax, back in the beginning position, for about 30 seconds.
9. Then do the getting up exercise, or simply continue with your exercises.

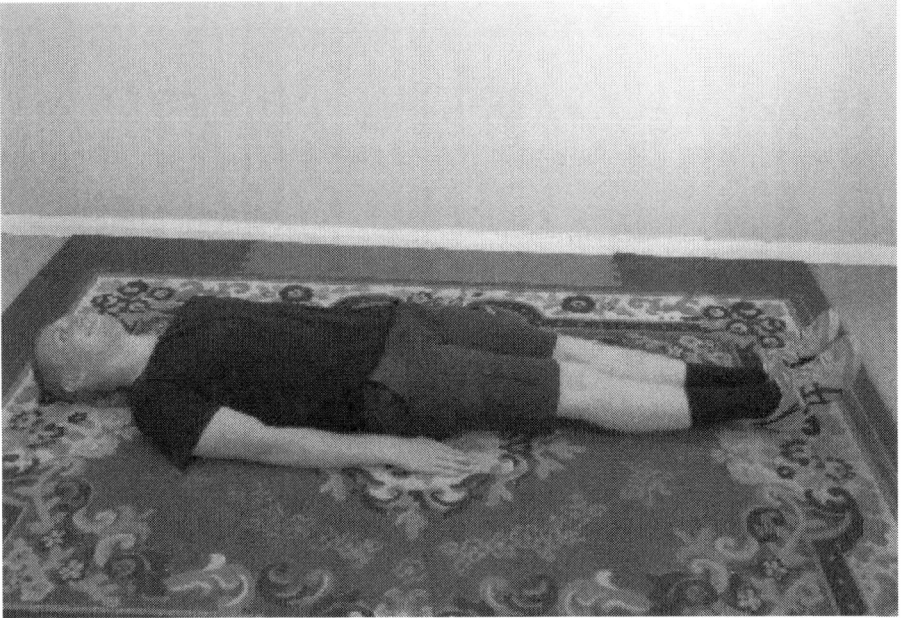

FIGURE 114

FIGURE 115

FIGURE 116

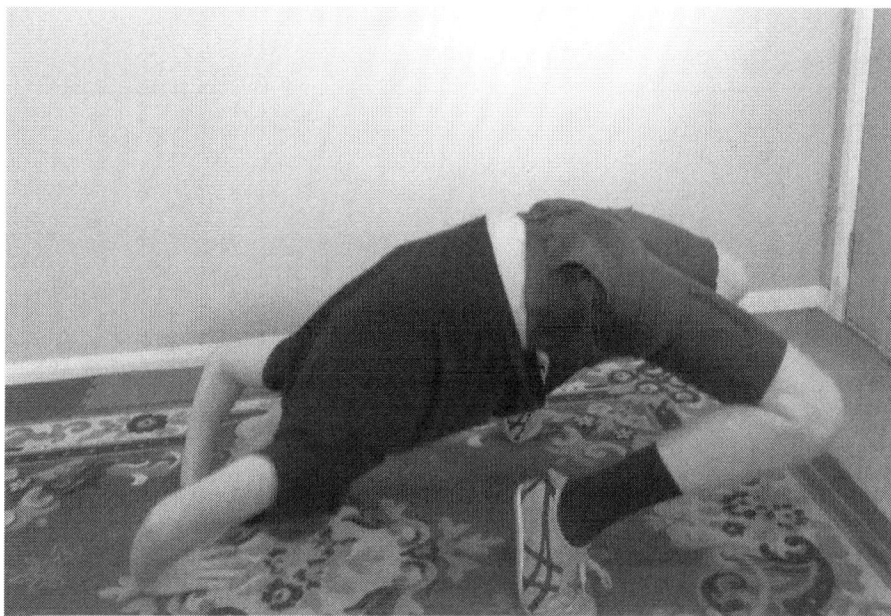

FIGURE 117

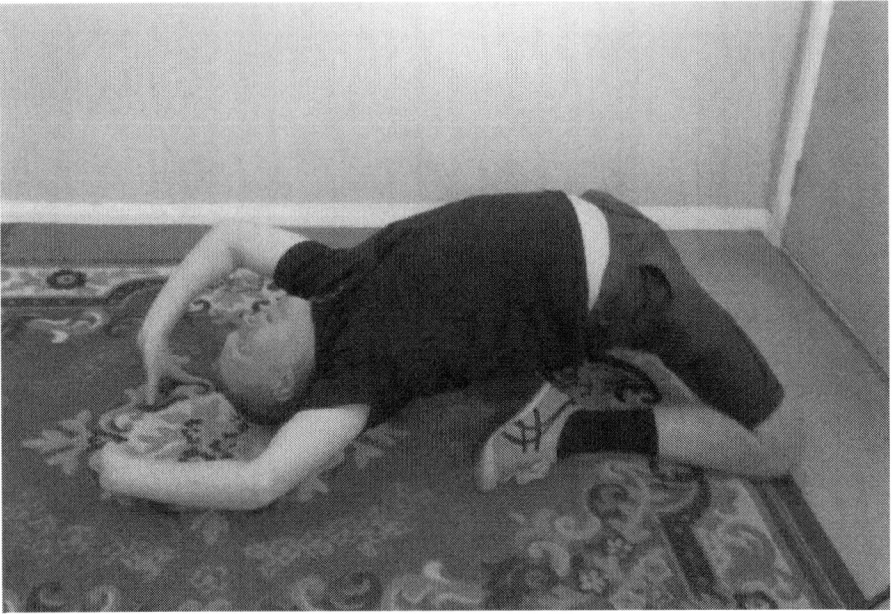

FIGURE 118

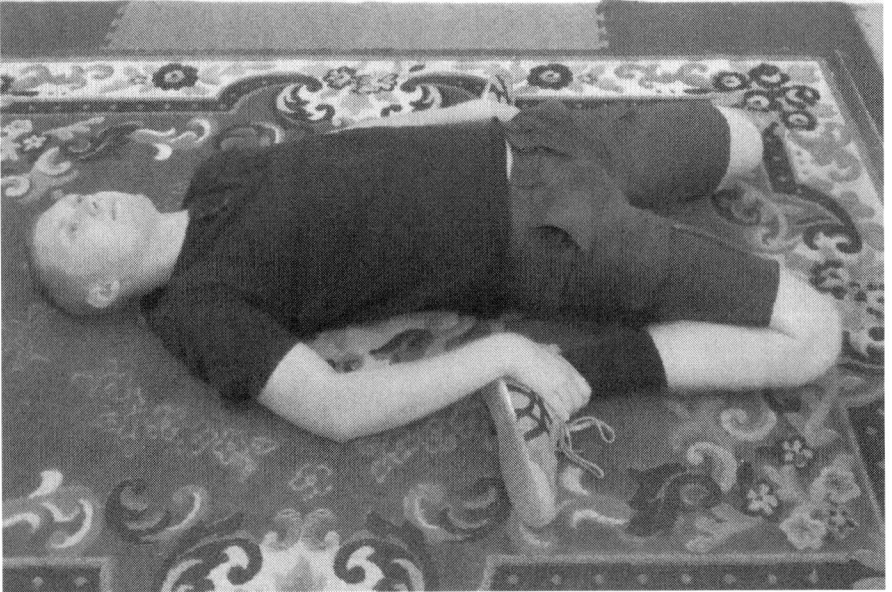

FIGURE 119

Part Six

Leg Stretches

Various versions of these exercises as given below are traditional to Yoga, Indian Martial Arts, Shaolin, Karate, Savate, and many other arts.

These are used in various guises by all martial arts. Again, Ving Tsun Kuen uses some, but rarely, and so at our school we have taken variations from Ving Tsun Kuen combined with Shaolin or other Martial Arts, or modified from Yoga. There are basically two kinds, ones done standing upright, and ones done on the ground.

Standing upright means there is a direct correspondence with the degree of stretch and the kick. Stretching on the ground loses about 25% of that correspondence when you stand up. That is why we mostly try to do the stretches standing up, when it can be done in relative safety.

We do these ones regularly:

- Side Stretch Waist bends.
- Inside, Outside, Inside Waist bends.
- Chin to Knees.
- Windmills.
- Left Leg Out and Down.
- Elbows, Feet, Behind (3-Corner Stretch.).

Side Stretch

1. Stand with your feet one shoulder width apart. (Figure 120).
2. Keep your feet parallel and to the front, with your knees straight, turn your shoulders to the left until they are at right angles to your feet. (Figure 121).
3. Bend towards your left knee, keeping your back straight, grab your ankle, and pull firmly. Pull your chin towards your feet, not your forehead to your knees. Grab your leg as far down as you can, then bend your elbows and pull, rather than keep your elbows straight. Keeping them straight is a push, not a pull, and uses the wrong muscles. Hold for ten seconds. (Figure 122).
4. Come completely up to vertical once more. Ensure that you keep facing at 90 degrees to your feet. (Figure 123).
5. Now turn completely around to your right while keeping your feet parallel and to the front. Do it like a robot. (Figure 124).
6. Bend down, again holding your ankle and pulling firmly the same as in "3" above, but towards the right knee instead of the left. (Figure 125).
7. Come completely up to vertical once more. Keep your facing at 90 degrees to your feet as you rise. (Same as Figure 124).
8. You have now completed one side stretch. You must do at least 2 more each side. Turn completely around to the left side. Repeat the points 1-7
9. After completing two more repetitions on each side, turn completely around to your right while keeping your feet parallel and to the front. Do it like a robot. (As in point 2 above, Figure 121).
10. Continue from point "3". Repeat for a total of 3 times each side.
11. After doing it 3 times you can go into the next one the "Inside Outside Stretch", or you can finish it off with the "Chin to Knees" exercise, Figures 141 and onwards.

This exercise is very good for the Ving Tsun Kuen side kick, which kicks with the side of the foot to the front while keeping your facing so you can hit the man with both hands, rather than to the side of the body like most side kicks. We also do the more usual side kick as well.

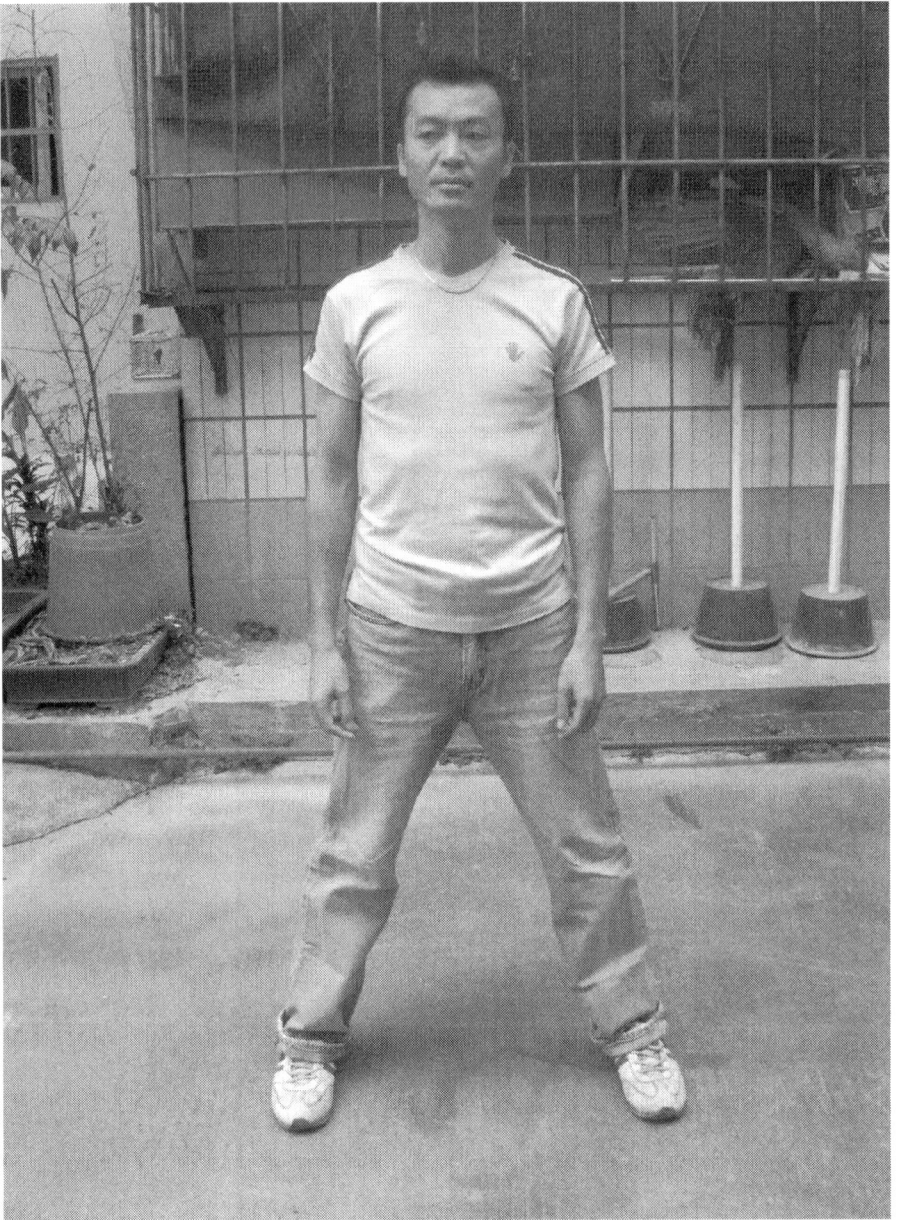

FIGURE 120

FIGURE 121

FIGURE 122

FIGURE 123

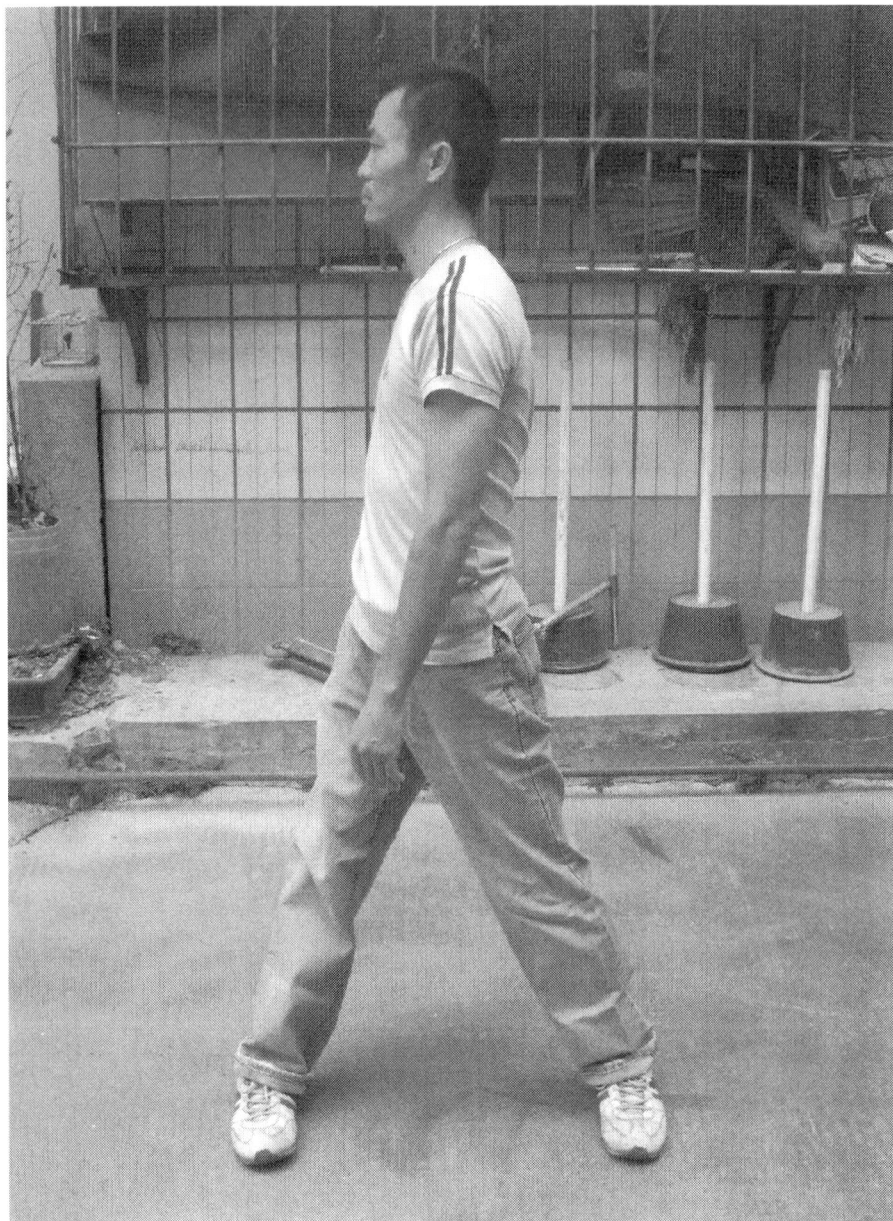

FIGURE 124

FIGURE 125

Outside, Inside, Outside Stretch

Each position is held for ten seconds. Do the left side and then the right side. This exercise is good for the waist, and is also good for improving kicks. This is usually done immediately after the above exercise, continuing from the last position in it.

1. Stand with feet a shoulder width apart. Keep your knees straight throughout the exercise. You should look like Figure 120 in the previous exercise, since this exercise usually follows that one immediately at the end, and this is the position you end up in.
2. Turn your left foot through ninety degrees. (Figure 126).
3. Then using your hands, grab your ankle and pull your right ear to the outside of your left knee and hold for 10 seconds. (Figure 127, 128). Keep your left leg completely straight at all times.
4. Come all the way up. (Figure 129).
5. Go down again this time to the INSIDE of the SAME leg. Pull your left ear to the inside of your left knee, grab and hold for 10 seconds. (Figures 130, 131).
6. Come all the way up. (Figure 132).
7. Go down again to the OUTSIDE of the SAME leg. (Figure 133).
8. Come all the way up. (Figure 134).
9. Using your waist, snap and face to the right side. (Figure 135).
10. Repeat the whole exercise on the other side.
11. First go to the OUTSIDE of your right knee. (Figure 136).
12. Come up. (Figure 137).
13. Go down to the INSIDE of your right knee. (Figure 138).

14. Come all the way up again. (Figure 139).
15. Go once more to the OUTSIDE of the right knee. (Figure 140).
16. Straighten up.
17. Put your feet together and face to the front, and finish with the "Chin to Knees" exercise. (Follow the Figures from 141 and 142 and the instructions on them.)

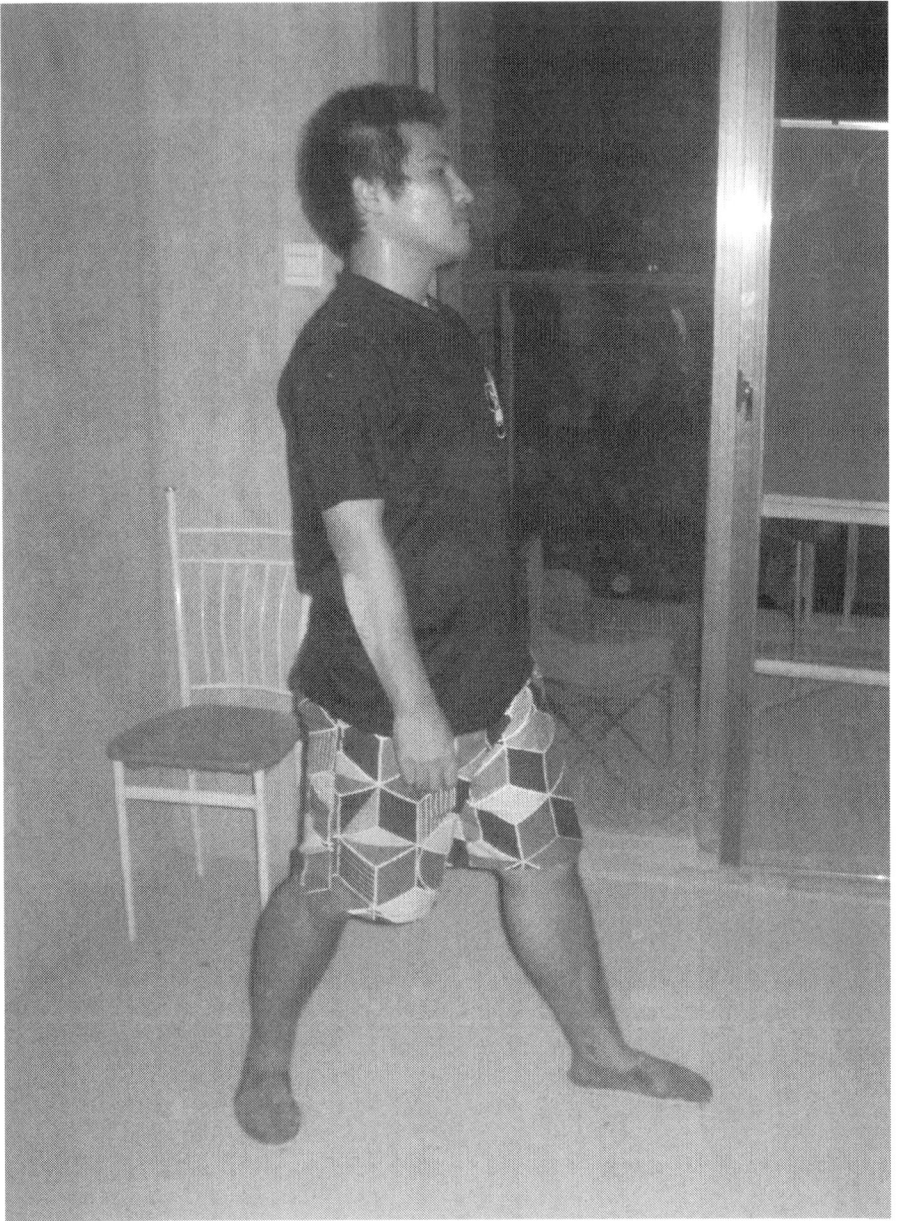

FIGURE 126

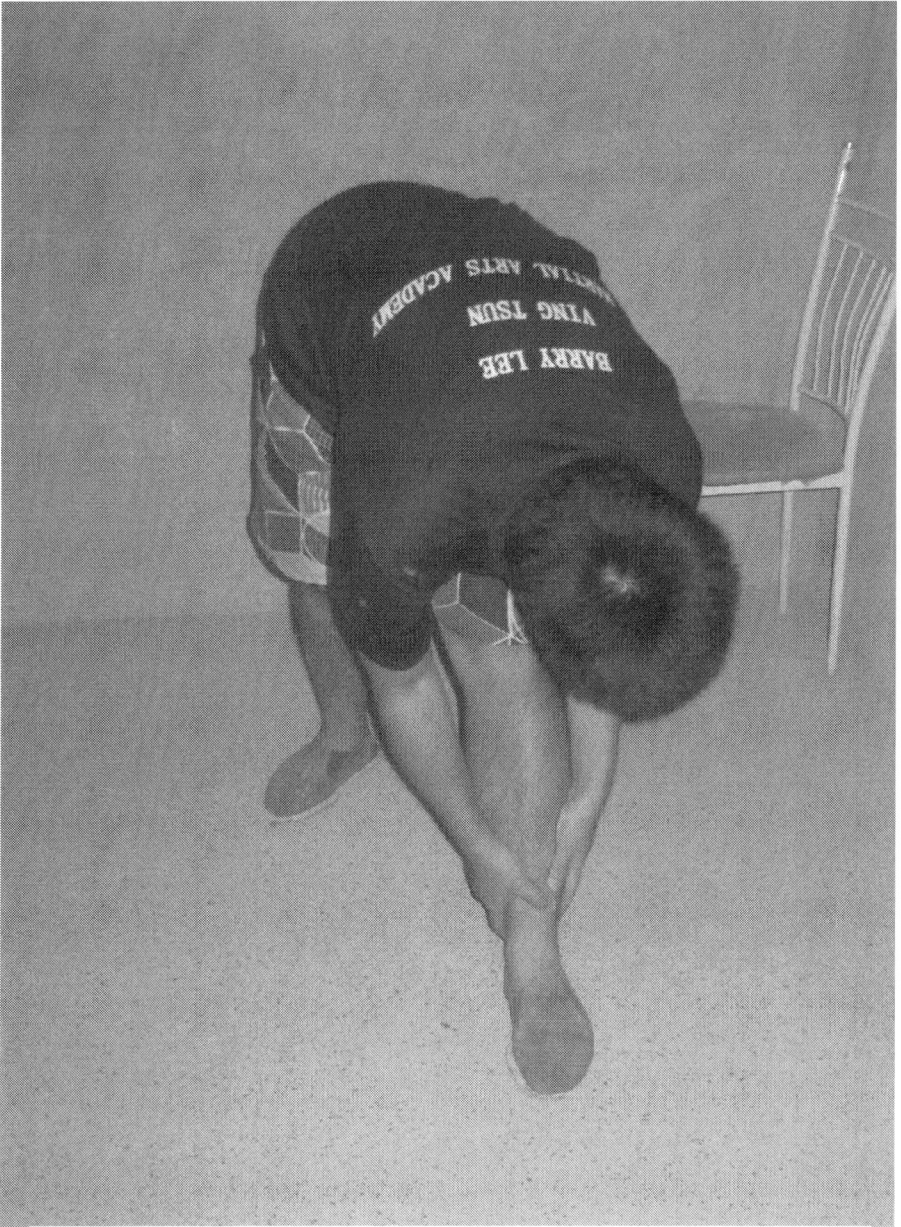

FIGURE 127

FIGURE 128

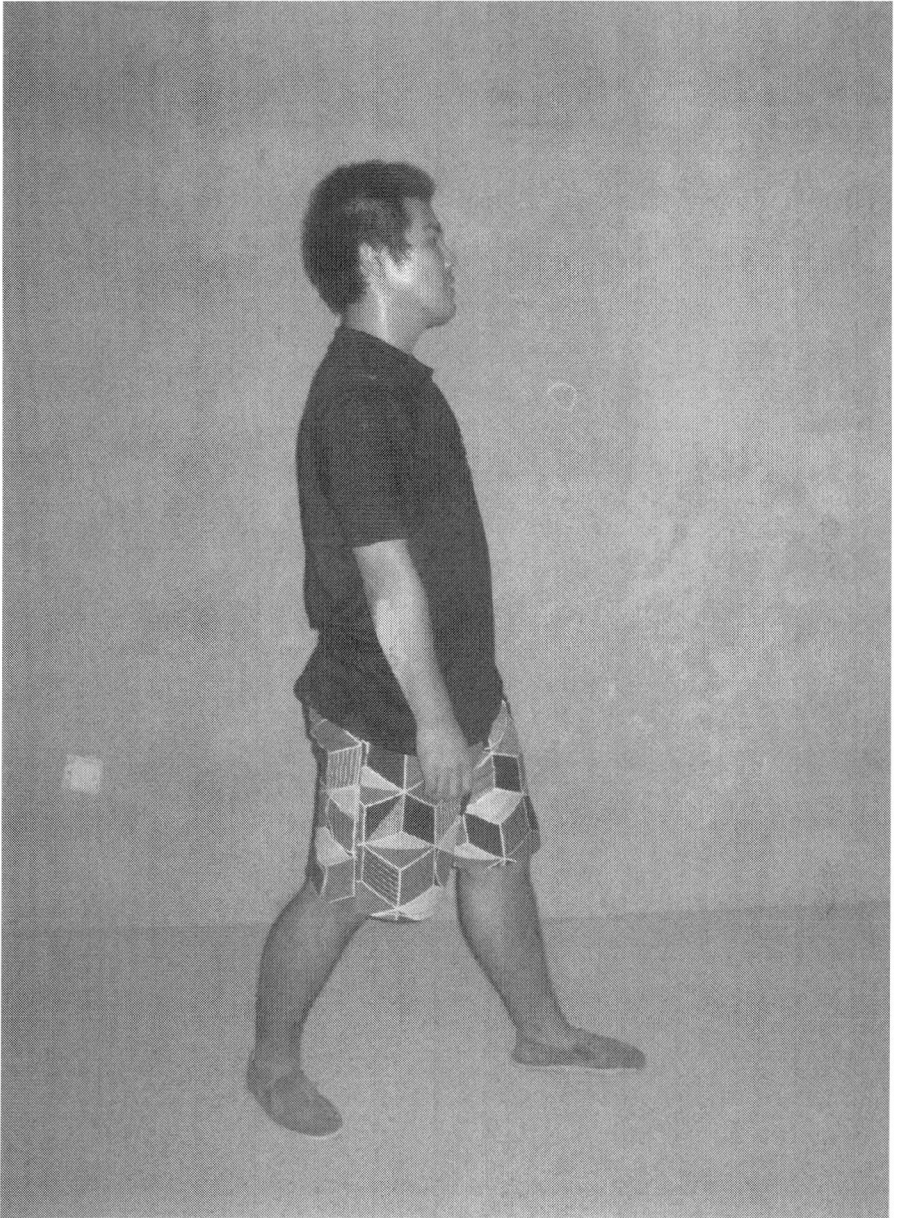

FIGURE 129

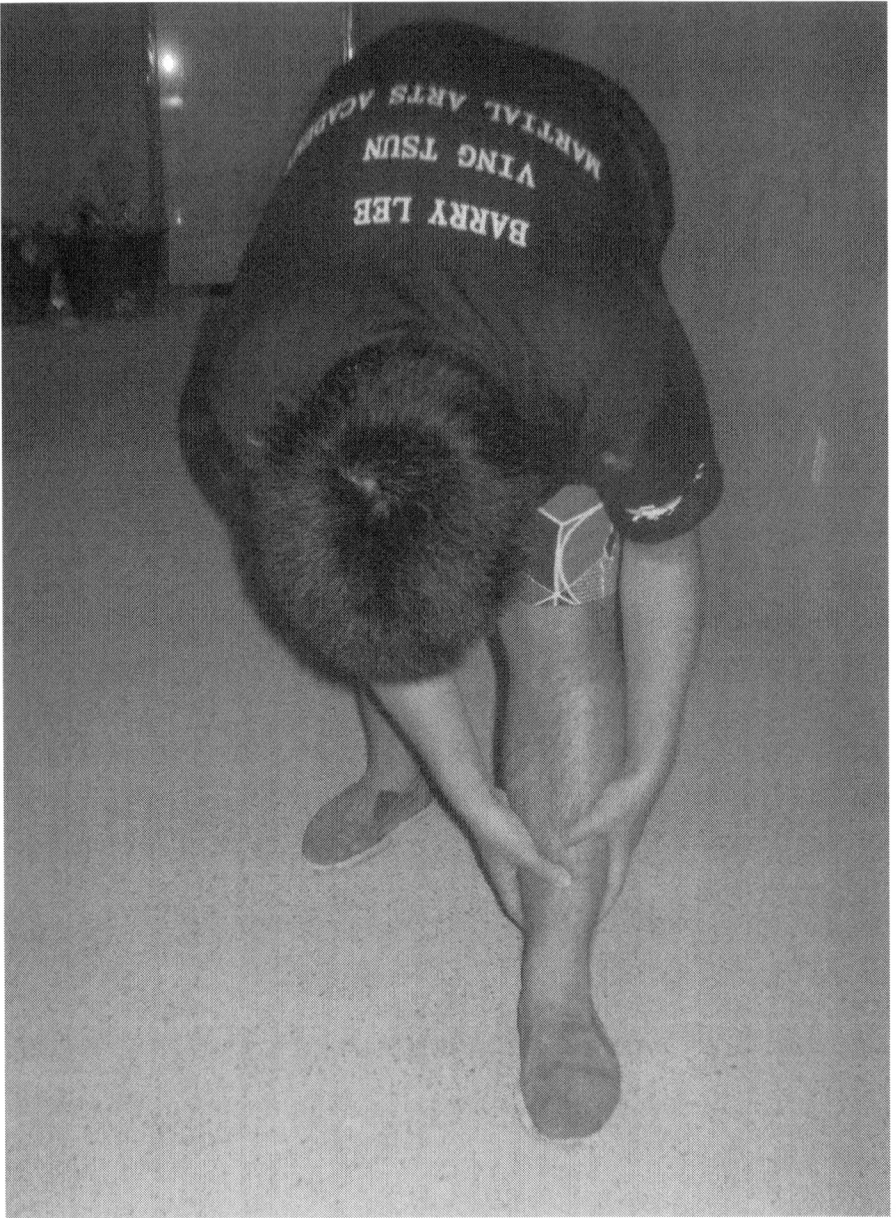

FIGURE 130

FIGURE 131

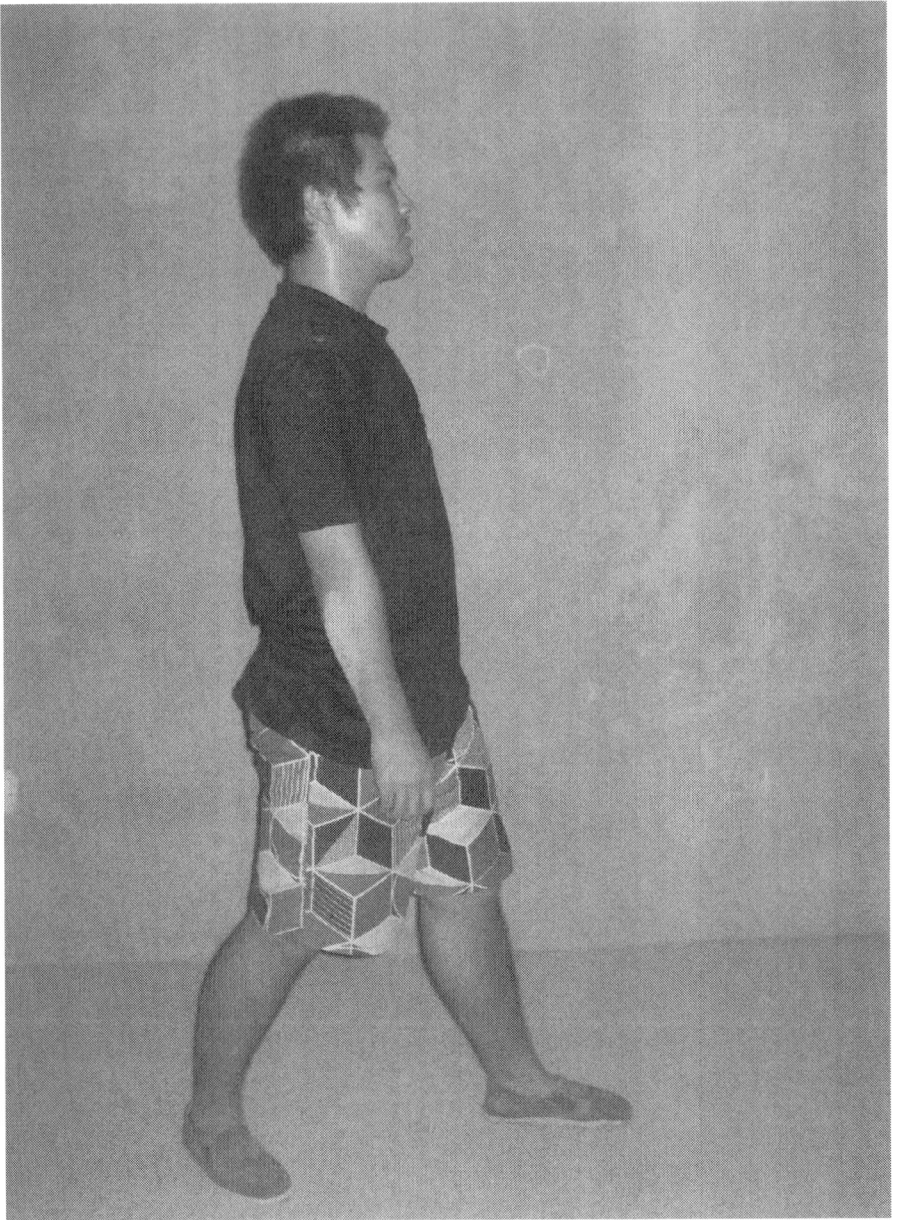

FIGURE 132

FIGURE 133

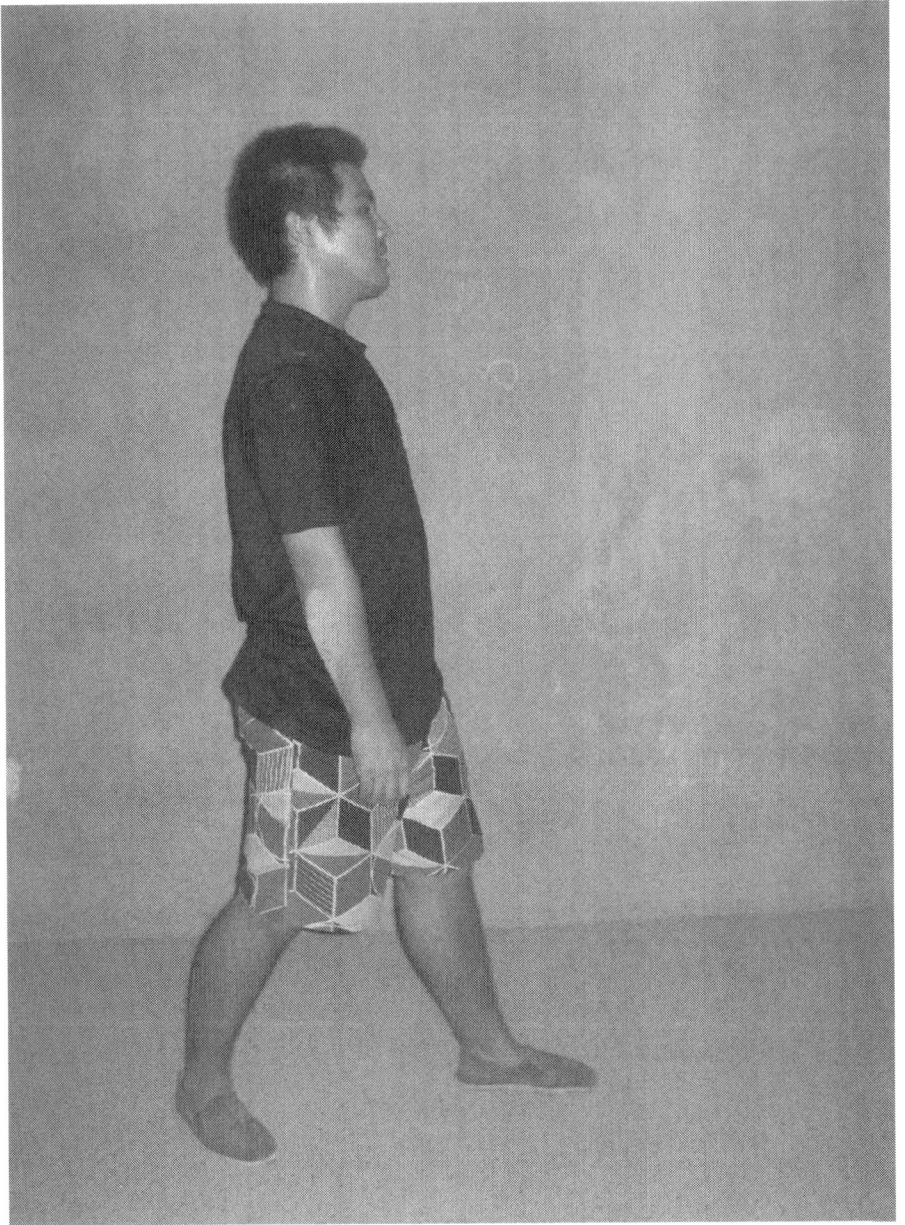

FIGURE 134

FIGURE 135

FIGURE 136

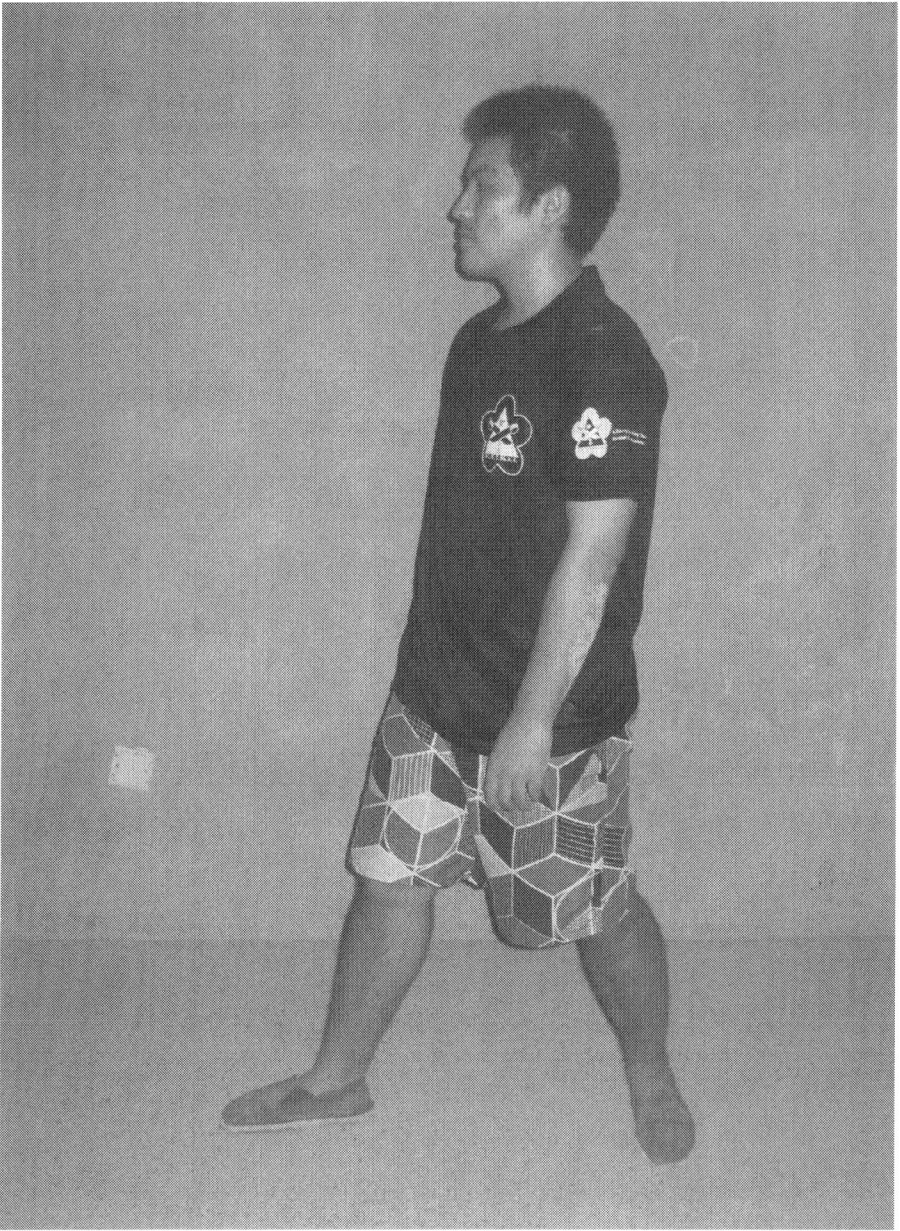

FIGURE 137

FIGURE 138

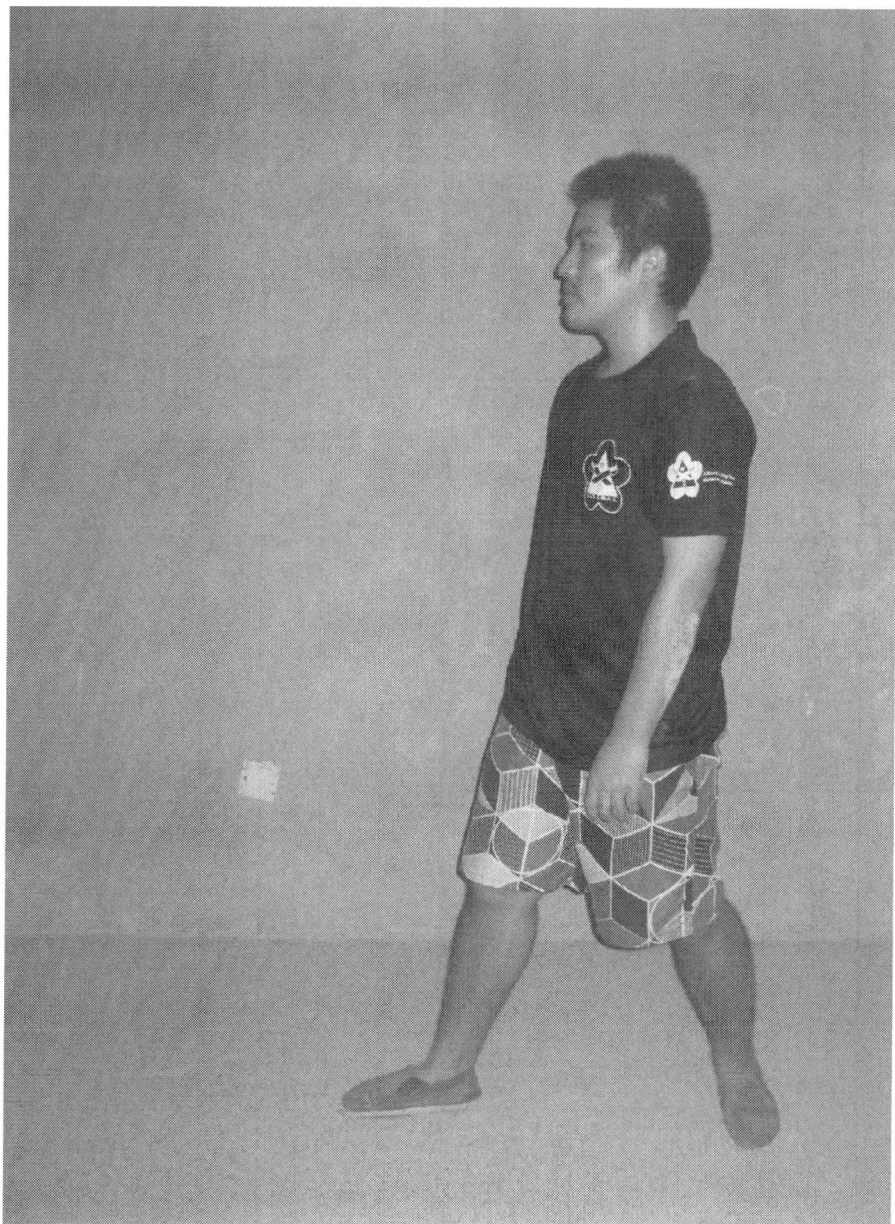

FIGURE 139

FIGURE 140

Chin to Knees

This is used a lot in Yoga and Hindu wrestlers, and other systems. We use it all the time to finish many of our other exercises. I put it here rather than in the Yoga section more because it is used separately at the end of our exercises than an exercise by itself.

1. Pull your feet together and push upwards and backwards with your hands over your head. (Figure 141).
2. Then bend down with knees straight, and grab your ankles and pull for twenty seconds. (Figure 142).
3. Bend your knees slightly and come up vertically, pushing upwards and back reaching for the sky with both hands, the same position the exercise was started in. (Back to Figure 141).

FIGURE 141

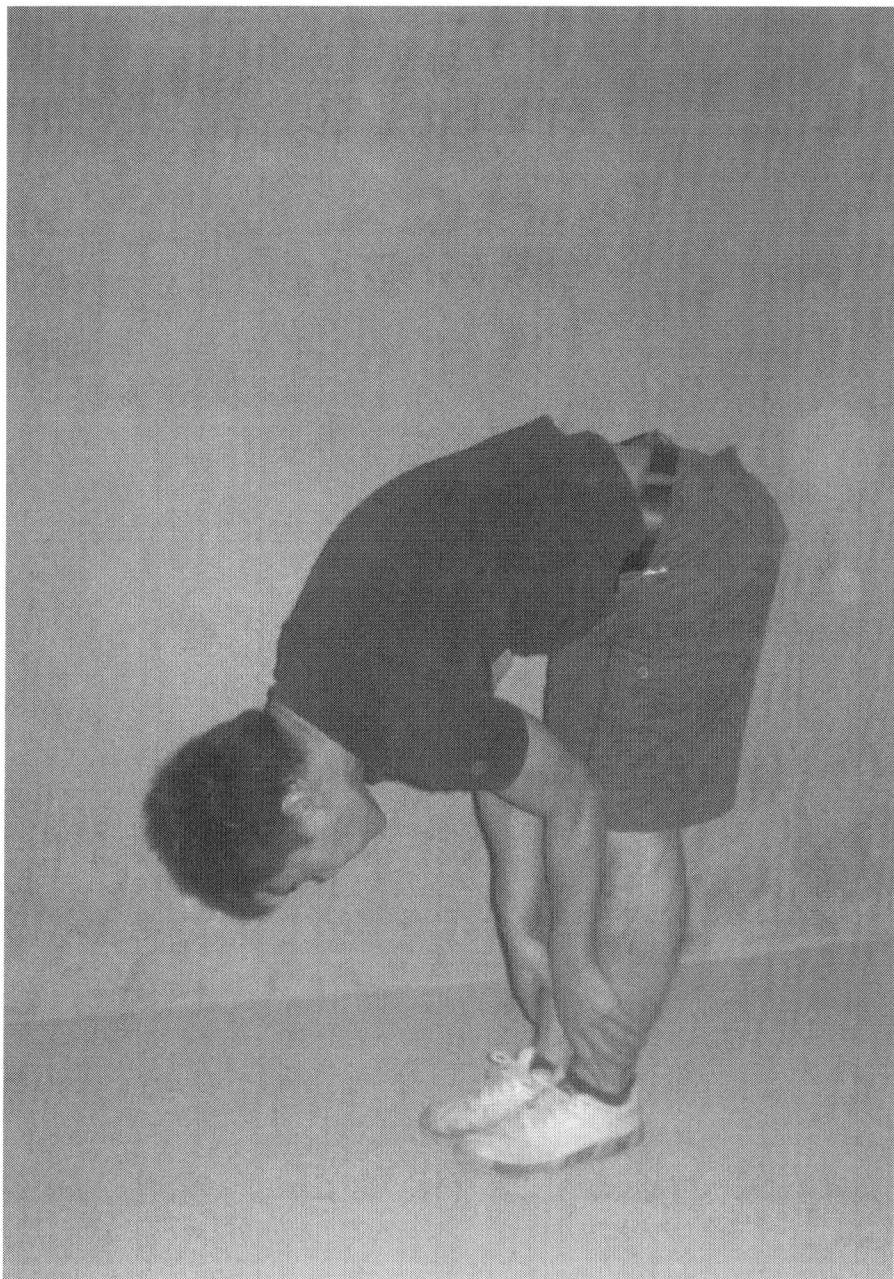

FIGURE 142

Windmills

1. Start with your feet a shoulder width apart.
2. Reach up to the sky with your right hand. (Figure 143).
3. Now bring your arm in an arc while you are turning to face your left side, and put your palm firmly on the ground beside your left leg. (Figure 144).
4. Extend your left arm and reach for the sky while coming up then turn to face the right-hand side once you are vertical. (Figure 145).
5. Bring your palm down firmly on the right-hand side of your right foot. (Figure 146).
6. Reach up to the sky with your right hand. (Figure 143) and you are back at the beginning to start a new cycle.
7. Each cycle reaches as far as you can around, in a circle, and you are supposed to try to slam the hand into the ground ballistically.

This should be repeated 20 times. It should be done powerfully, at first slowly then increasing in speed. It increases all kinds of linear power, and increases the stretch and power of your waist and legs for kicking. The exercise "Inside, Outside, Inside" should immediately follow.

This exercise can be a bit risky and difficult for unfit people, and should be aimed at those who have had enough body conditioning to be able to take the strain.

FIGURE 143

FIGURE 144

FIGURE 145

205

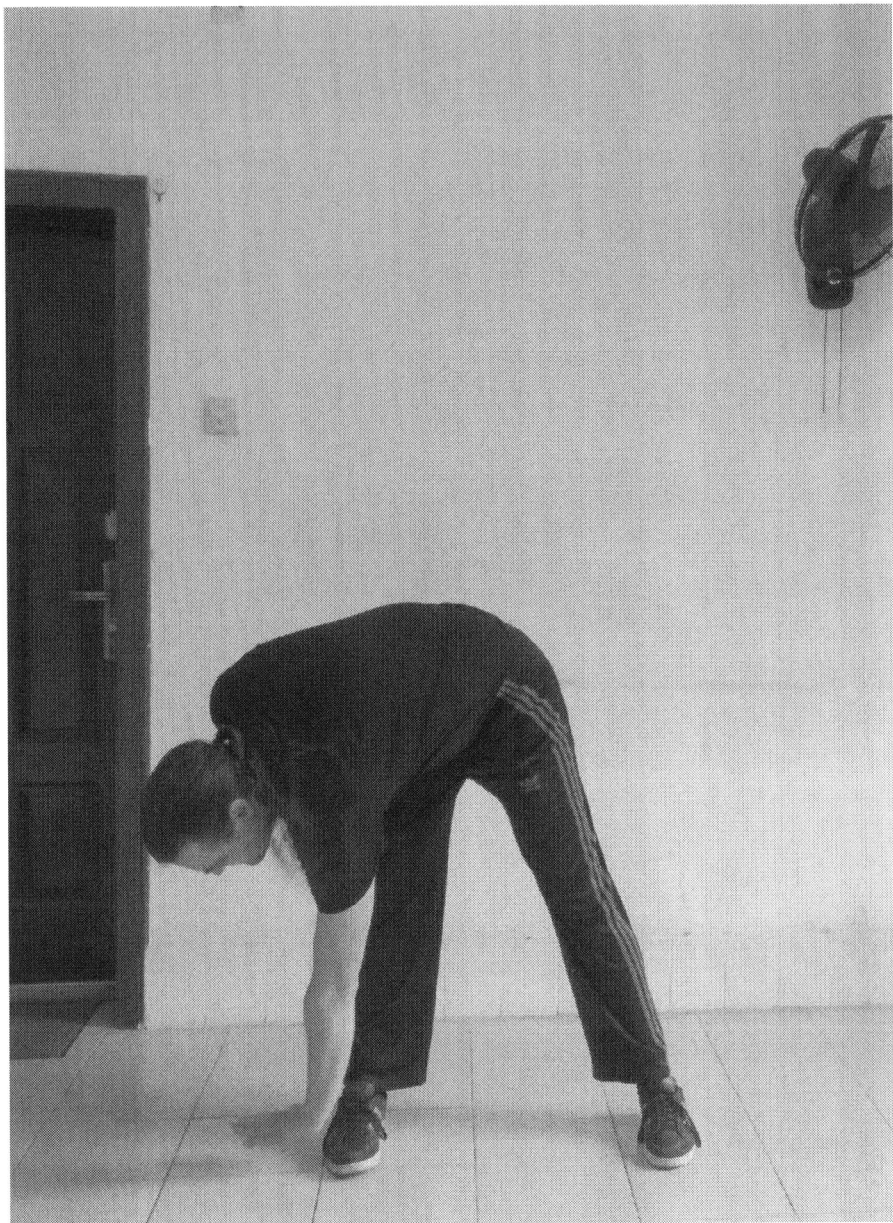

FIGURE 146

Left Leg Out and Down

Left leg out, toes to ceiling, side, sole to ground. 3 Reps Per Side. This exercise is extremely good for all the various kicks in Ving Tsun Kuen. This version is a traditional Shaolin exercise. Variations are used by many martial arts.

1. Put out your left leg, and bend your left foot back so the toes aim at the ceiling. Let your left heel slide out and bend your right leg until your right knee is over your waist, and outside of your right shoulder. Your left calf should be almost on the floor, and you should be pushing your left heel out. Your supporting foot should be flat on the floor. (Figure 147). Push out for a few seconds. Pull your toes back, and shape it like a front heel kick. Count to ten.
2. Roll your left foot over so the inside ankle is flat to the floor. (Figure 148). Push out for a few seconds. Pull your toes back, and shape it like a front heel kick. Count to ten.
3. Roll your foot down so the sole is flat to the floor. The edge of the foot should be outwards and the toes pulled back, like a side kick. (Figure 149). Push out for a few seconds. Count to ten.
4. Now change sides, staying as close to the ground as possible. Don't rise up as you change at all, but kind of snake close to the ground. (Figure 150). Your weight will shift from your right foot to your left, as you move your body from the right to the left.
5. You should end up with your toes pointing to the ceiling, as at the beginning of the previous side. (Figure 151). Count to ten.
6. Repeat all the steps.
7. Push out, roll side of the foot to the floor. (Figure 152). Count to ten.
8. Push, roll foot flat to the floor. (Figure 153). Count to ten.
9. Change staying low. (Same as Figure 150, only moving in the other direction, from left to right).

10. Point your toes to the ceiling. You should now be in the same position as number 1. (Figure 147). This is the end of one cycle, one repetition on each side.
11. Repeat twice more each side.
12. At the last change – don't move your feet. You can move straight into the next exercise or stand up, leaving your feet where they are, and move directly from this exercise into the "50 Punches, Wide Stance" exercise, or finish with the "Chin to Knees" exercise.

This is good for kicks, and leg and waist flexibility, and holds the positions for 3 of our main kicking shapes.

FIGURE 147

FIGURE 148

FIGURE 149

FIGURE 150

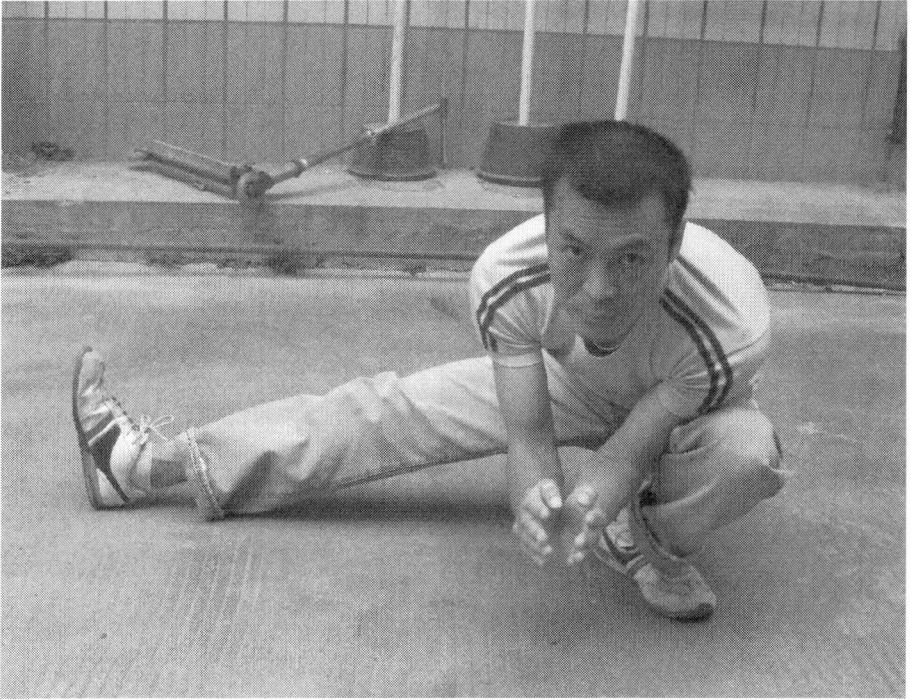

FIGURE 151

FIGURE 152

FIGURE 153

Elbows, Feet, Behind

Also called the 3-corner stretch.

This is good for kicks, and leg and waist flexibility, and good for shoulders. This is a variation based on Shaolin exercises.

1. Spread your feet a slightly uncomfortable distance apart.
2. Bending down, reach your elbows towards the ground. (Figure 154).
3. Now reach with the heels of your hands to your feet. (Figure 155).
4. Now reach with the heels of your hands to the floor between and behind your legs. (Figure 156).
5. Repeat 20 times, reaching and stretching. Don't bounce, just reach.
6. At the end, put your hands on the ground under your shoulders. (Figure 157).
7. Bring your elbows together and put them on the ground between your feet and stretch some more. (Figure 158).
8. Straighten your arms again. (Figure 159).
9. Now bring your feet together behind your hands. (Figure 160).
10. Pull your chin to your knees same as the middle of "Chin to Knees" exercise, Figure 142).
11. Slightly bend your knees to take the strain off your back.
12. Rising vertically, reach up and back. (Same as Figure 141).

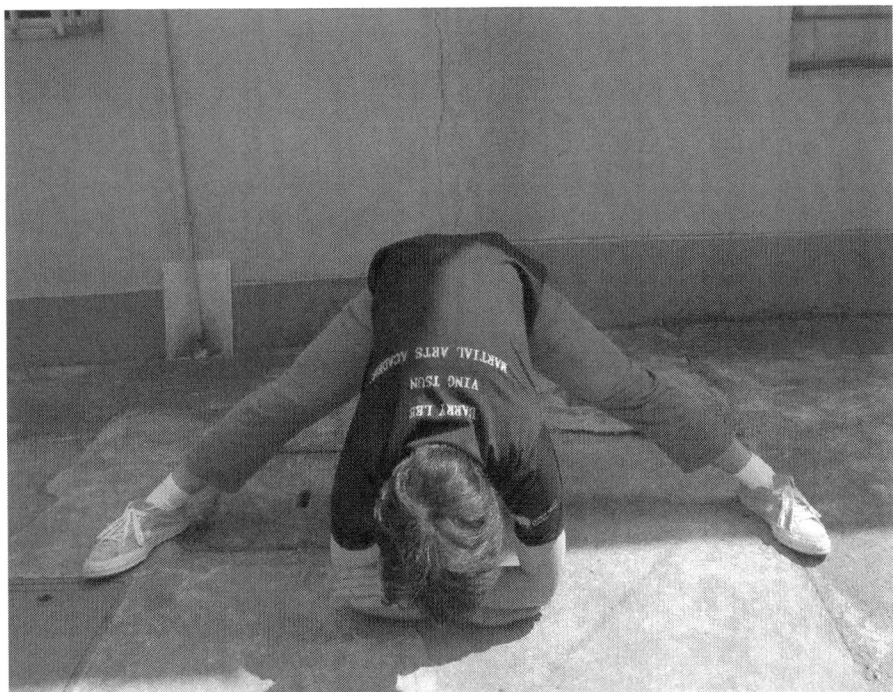

FIGURE 154

FIGURE 155

FIGURE 156

FIGURE 157

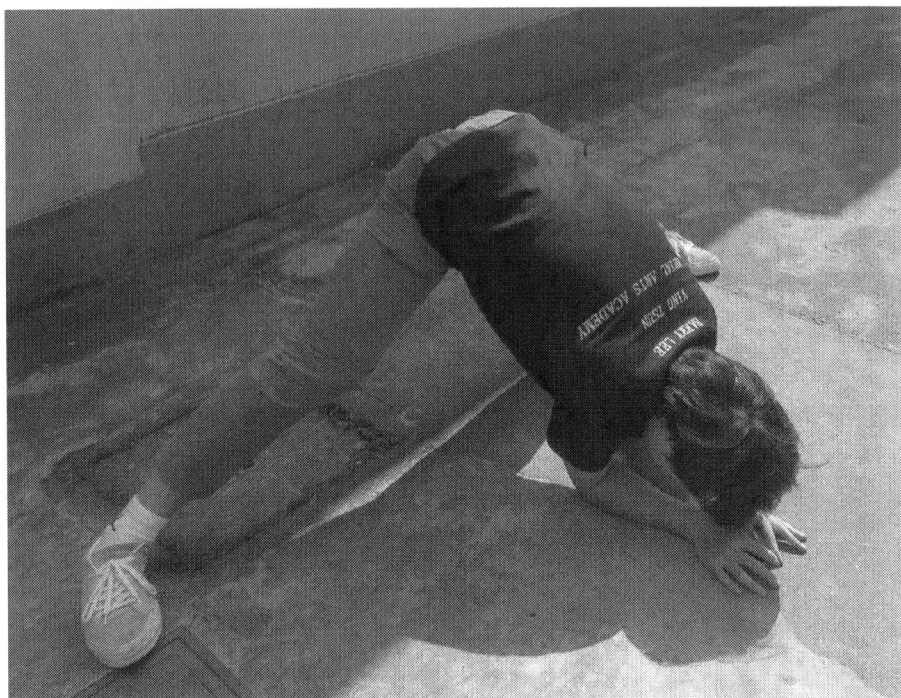

FIGURE 158

FIGURE 159

216

FIGURE 160

Appendices

Short Exercise Program

Notes

1. What follows is a good overall program using both traditional and non-traditional exercises from the above lists: **Print it out, stick it on the wall.**

2. The exercises marked with an asterisk (*) are those that would be a bare minimum to do each day.

3. Beginners should take it easy and take their time with the exercises, doing them slowly and carefully, but as correctly as possible. This is to reduce the chance of injury and to teach the muscles how to move and the positions they should be in, and to stretch them just a little more every day. More advanced people should get faster and faster, until they can cover this list in about 10 or 15 minutes.

4. If you are doing it on your own, ensure that you are doing the exercises right, or you might hurt yourself.

5. Often the exercises can be done with the first few slowly and lightly, building up power and speed towards the end of the repetitions.

6. If you exercise in the morning, your flexibility is lower, so do the stretches slowly and stretch less distance than normal. Mornings are more suitable for form work and slow self-training than hard exercise. Evenings, the reverse is true. You can stretch more, and your body can move faster. Lunchtime training should avoid exhausting exercises like running, but these exercises given in this list can be done both morning and evening, although running other than short sprints do not really help fighting or learning Ving Tsun Kuen.

7. The order and content can be varied at need, but if you change things, try to substitute exercises that do the same things.

8. Any pre-existing conditions or injuries should be allowed for in any exercise program. Take it easy until you know you can handle it, building up slowly to full power and speed. If there are any doubts, consult your doctor.

9. There is also a 'cooldown' which was done in the last few minutes of the class.

Exercises

1. *Jumping on the Spot for 2-5 minutes, followed by a ten-second walk.
2. Knee Raises, and Hindu Squats. *30-50 knee raises to chest, followed by half that in flat-footed squats, followed by a ten-second walk. Increase repetitions for advanced students.
3. Windmills 20 repetitions. These can be done slowly as a stretch. Can be left out for beginners.
4. *Elbows, Feet, Behind. 20 repetitions.
5. *Waist Bends, with feet parallel, one shoulder width apart, hold for 10 seconds. 3 repetitions each side.
6. *Outside, Inside, Outside Stretch. Turn your foot 90°, bend waist. Outside, inside, outside 10 seconds each side.
7. Feet together, Chin to Knees, 30 seconds.
8. *3 corner stretch.
9. *50 Hard Punches in Wide Stance.
10. *2-4 types of abdominal exercises, such as 50 short crunches, 5 slow leg lifting exercises, 30 full sit-ups, 20 L-R sit-ups ("Jacky Chans" or "Boxing sit-ups", 20 "Rowing" sit-ups, holding up legs for 30 seconds 3 repetitions, 10 half crunches repetitions, etc.
11. Face Down Plank. Elbows on the ground pushing forwards for 30 seconds or 1 minute.
12. Triceps Dips "reverse push ups" 3 repetitions slowly.
13. *Getting Up Exercise - 5 repetitions.
14. 5-10 "Sun Asana" yoga exercises, some slowly and some fast. With or without variations
15. *Elbow Press.
16. *Elbow Stretch.
17. *"Back Forward Back, Cross Behind Cross".
18. *Arm Rotations. Circling, crossing at the elbow, ten each direction, full range of movement. Also, this can be done to revive tired arms after vigorous Chi Sau practice.
19. Have a drink of water, and a brief rest before you start Siu Lim Tao. Remember to re-hydrate frequently, especially in hot weather.

Cool Down

At the end of class, we would then go through this list of exercises to finish off the training session.

1. 50 hard punches.
2. Variety punches.
3. 50 light and loose punches.
4. Arm Rotations. (Including variations on occasion).
5. We would then bow out and finish the class.

About the Author

~ Antisthenes, Ancient Greek scholar.

Bill Dowding was born in 1957 and currently lives in NSW, Australia. He didn't discover martial arts until he was 13, and studied Western Boxing and Judo briefly. When he was 15, he saw some Martial Arts tv shows and movies, and since he couldn't find any kind of Chinese Martial Arts that was useful for fighting, started formal training in a kind of Shotokan-based Karate which he studied until he was nearly 18. He entered competitions, performing against and with black belts which in those days were serious competitions. His best was for a team that came 3rd place at state level. When 17 he sparred against his very close friend Toni Bardakos who had practiced Ving Tsun Kuen for only six months at the time, and was easily beaten. He resolved to change to Ving Tsun Kuen but this style was extremely hard to find – he had to move to Sydney, but was still in his final year of school. He did a little exchanging of techniques with Toni Bardakos off and on for the rest of the year, then moved to Sydney on Christmas day 1975, and waited until the studio opened for business after the Christmas break, January 1976. His first Ving Tsun Kuen teacher was Greg Choi, a direct student of Yip Man. Later Bill went to University in New England, and studied some Tae Kwon Do and exchanged techniques with a few other martial artists, in styles such as White Crane, Hsing I and Tong Long (Southern Mantis).

Over the coming years, he practiced with many teachers, still searching for the ideal style, toying with the Bruce Lee concept of "absorbing what is useful" (a concept and interpretation he now considers ludicrous.)

He again studied Tong Long, but again it was yet another system, before returning to Ving Tsun once more.

Toni Bardakos changed Ving Tsun Kuen systems to Chu Shong Tin's Wing Chun system under Jim Fung. Bill moved again to Sydney and practiced a lot under this system with Toni, for a few years, until he was able to teach, although "unofficially" since he disliked gradings.

He taught Ving Tsun Kuen at University while getting his Science degree. (Biochemistry and Physiology with Psychology as a minor – the first of several qualifications including Systems Analysis and Design, and qualifications from the Australian Institute of Sport.) He also taught self-defence and women's self-defence classes for a few years, until one day Alan Au-Yeung, a student of Barry Lee, walked into his studio in 1989.

This changed everything.

He took one look at the Wong Shun Leung system, and the first question Bill asked Barry Lee, his new and first real sifu was "How do you want me to stand?" He started from scratch, learning everything anew, discarding the old as comparatively useless. This was in 1989.

Over the next decade or so he trained hard, exclusively in the Barry Lee system, except for his hobby of medieval combat. He has been training extensively since then, including running schools in this method, attending the first and second world conferences in HK in 1999 and 2005, and the opening of the Yip Man Museum in 2002 as a member of this system. During this time, he also obtained black belts in Arnis, and a bridging course for instructors in Jiu Jitsu that sort of lead up to black belt. He also travelled extensively in Europe, exchanging ideas with other teachers in several countries, including helping Barry Lee train some students in Germany and other European countries.

He is also friends with the people who learned Ving Tsun Kuen with Bruce Lee under Yip Man in Hong Kong, and still sees them regularly in his trips to Hong Kong and China. He was friends with Yip Man's earliest students Kwok Fu and Lun Gai in Guangdong Foshan, and continued these friendships until they passed away.

He also spent some time teaching other martial arts systems how to defend against knives as a speciality. He also travelled teaching in several European countries including Denmark, Germany and England, both teaching VTK and extensively studying European weaponry in the nineties. He studied European weaponry for more than two decades, beginning his interest during his university years.

He has also travelled extensively in China, exchanging teaching methods with many lineages of Ving Tsun Kuen and its related styles. While living in China, he began studying his tenth formal martial art, Yang Tai Chi. He has students in the UK, Holland, Germany, and Australia, as well as in China, where he lived for over nine years before returning to Australia, where he lives currently. All the schools are small and exclusive because he is someone who doesn't seek publicity, nor seeks to create large schools of low-quality students simply to make money. Real Kung Fu is not about fame and fortune, but about the quality of the students.

He has taught security forces in Australia, China, and from several European countries, as well as some military personnel, including some special forces. He is on the Australian Defence Force list of approved instructors. He travels regularly to Europe and China where he is a consultant for many schools in keeping up their standards of training.

Bill has also been involved with security, teaching self-defence at universities and for private companies and security agencies, as well as advisor to Olympic team members. He has also had opportunities to test the system in real use, as well as 'contests' with other martial artists.

He has lectured in the psychology of violence at University level, being nominated as a research associate for his work in this area, and published, interviewed on radio, and/or filmed for TV, in Australia, China, Hong Kong and other countries, in Chinese and German as well as English. He lived and taught in China, and teaching culture, writing and history at the Guangxi University of Chinese Medicine in Southern China as an English Professor. His Ving Tsun Kuen school in Nanning, Guangxi, China is the oldest school of this style in the province, and recently is now teaching in Shanghai as well.

He has also recently lectured on the health aspects of Traditional Chinese Martial Arts at the Guangxi University of Chinese Medicine Research Hospital, Nanning, Guangxi, China.

He has been writing for decades. He has won national prizes in science fiction, published in various magazines from Science Fiction, Food and Wine and Travel magazines, to, naturally, several national and international martial arts magazines. His Science Fiction stories have also been published in a book on local Speculative Fiction. One of the plays he co-wrote with his brother was performed to critical acclaim.

He is currently in production of several books on various aspects of Ving Tsun Kuen, plus some children's books and a Science Fiction anthology.

Printed in Great Britain
by Amazon